THE ROMANCE OF PREACHING

C. Silvester Horne

The Romance of Preaching

By
CHARLES SILVESTER HORNE

With an Introduction by
CHARLES R. BROWN, D. D.

And a Biographical Sketch by
HOWARD A. BRIDGMAN, D. D.

NEW YORK   CHICAGO   TORONTO
Fleming H. Revell Company
LONDON   AND   EDINBURGH

Copyright, 1914, by
FLEMING H. REVELL COMPANY

New York: 158 Fifth Avenue
Chicago: 125 North Wabash Ave.
Toronto: 25 Richmond Street, W.
London: 21 Paternoster Square
Edinburgh: 100 Princes Street

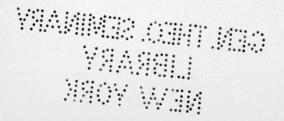

Preface

TO many of my husband's friends these lectures will come with a special message. They were much on his mind and heart, and before leaving England he spent many hours in their preparation. His affection for the American people had always been strong, and when the invitation came to him to deliver the Divinity Lectures at Yale University, he felt that it was an honour impossible to refuse, though the need for a complete rest was overwhelming. Into their delivery he put all the fire and enthusiasm that were so characteristic of him, and the testimony on all sides was that never before had the lecturer so gripped his audience, and so won all by his personality. Afterwards many of those who had heard him wrote to say how wonderful had been the help and uplift, and how in difficult places they would gain constant inspiration from his words.

Three days after the last lecture he was called suddenly to the presence of the Master whom he served so faithfully. My earnest hope is, that his last message may still cheer and help many of his brother ministers whom he loved so well, and for whom he gave his best.

KATHARINE M. HORNE.

Church Stretton,
August, 1914.

Introduction

By Charles R. Brown, D. D., Dean of the Yale Divinity School

FROM the days when Henry Ward Beecher gave the first series of lectures on the "Lyman Beecher Foundation" in Yale University, on through those years when this service has been performed by such eminent men as Phillips Brooks and R. W. Dale, Henry van Dyke and John Watson, Lyman Abbott and George A. Gordon, Washington Gladden and Francis G. Peabody, the task of inspiring young ministers to nobler effort in their high calling has been well performed. But among them all, few lecturers have ever so gripped the divinity students, the larger audience of pastors in active service and the thoughtful people of New Haven as did Silvester Horne when he spoke to us on "The Romance of Preaching."

He was himself a shining example of those

5

high and chivalrous qualities which he would covet for the true prophet, and the younger Knights of the Cross responded to his spiritual appeal as to the bugle-call of a genuine leader.

The intellectual distinction which marked his utterances, the fine literary form in which they were phrased, the moral passion which gave to their delivery that energy which belongs to words which are " spirit and life," together with the rare spiritual insight displayed, all combined to make notable the service rendered by Mr. Horne to Yale University.

It seemed tragic that just three days after he had finished this course of lectures, he should suddenly be caught away like the prophet of old, from the deck of a steamer as he neared the city of Toronto where he was to preach next day at the University. Here, indeed, are his last words, spoken in an upper room to his brother ministers, younger and older, upon whom he had breathed his own spirit of intense devotion to the high task of proclaiming the Gospel of Christ !

The sense of loss to England and to America, and to the whole Christian world, made all hearts heavy. But "he being dead yet speaketh," in these inspiring words and in that genius for friendship which has left its benediction upon so many thousands of hearts, and in that distinguished service which it was his privilege to render to Church and to State on that side the water and on this.

Yale University.

A Biographical Sketch

By Howard A. Bridgman, D. D., Editor of
" The Congregationalist "

INTO the forty-nine years of his earthly
life Charles Silvester Horne poured a
measure of service in behalf of his nation, his church and the world at large, such
as can be credited to few of his contemporaries on either side of the Atlantic. He was
fortunate in his ancestry, his training, his
environment, his family, his friends, and in
the opportunities that, from time to time,
crossed his path, but the greatest of God's
many gifts to him was a sense of the glory
and seriousness of life and an eagerness,
with God's help, to do his own part in the
work of the world. A son of the manse he
was born in Cuckfield, Sussex, England,
April 15, 1865, took his arts course at Glas-
gow University, entering upon graduation
the newly established theological school at
Oxford known as Mansfield College, whose

9

principal, the late Dr. Andrew M. Fairbairn, was renowned for his learning and his personal influence over his pupils. Before the young theologue, who at once evinced his unusual qualifications for the ministry, completed his course, a church in London claimed him as its leader and there at Kensington for ten years in a fashionable section of the world's metropolis Mr. Horne preached and laboured, building up a compact and vigorous organization and gaining distinction even in his earliest years as a pulpit and platform orator. Then came the pull on his sensitive, daring nature of London's poverty and need. Leaving his attractive pastorate, where he had won popularity among all classes, he went to Whitefield's Central Mission which stands in Tottenham Court Road, close to the homes of the poor and to haunts of shame. Into this new enterprise he entered with characteristic zeal and soon developed a great church of the institutional type, pervaded with a homelike atmosphere and ministering Sundays and week days alike to clerks, artisans and other types of working people, and exercising a beneficent influence over the neighbourhood, which sadly needed something to counteract the influence of the gin-house and brothel.

Meanwhile the Congregational Churches of England, and the Free Churches generally, had been claiming Mr. Horne's efficient assistance in the support of important enterprises. Invitations to speak here and there were showered upon him. He was honoured with the chairmanship of the Congregational Union of England and Wales. Pressing public issues like the controversy over the Education Bill drew him into the arena of politics, and he became known as one of the most gallant and earnest fighters for freedom in Church and State. His rare oratorical gifts made him one of the favourite spokesmen of the Non-conformist conscience on many public occasions. It was natural, in view of the reliance placed upon him, that he should at last yield to the strong demand that he stand for Parliament, and in 1910 he was returned as junior Member for Ipswich. For a time he undertook to carry

the burden of his great church along with his
Parliamentary duties, but at the end of ten
years of the hardest kind of work at Whitefield's he relinquished his leadership, only,
however, to give himself more untiringly to
clamorous calls for his services. He felt
especially the appeal of the Brotherhood
Movement, and was planning as National
President to give much time to its advocacy
and to details of administration.

All through the years of active ministry he
wielded a facile pen and many articles in
newspapers and magazines bear witness to
his literary fertility, while even more sub-
stantial and enduring in their influence are
his valuable volumes, " A Popular History of
the Free Churches," " A Modern Heretic,"
" A Story of the London Missionary Society,"
" The Ministry of the Modern Church," and
" David Livingstone." His last and in
many respects his noblest literary production
was the Lyman Beecher lectures at Yale, to
the preparation of which he devoted much
time during the last year of his life, and
which are embodied in this volume.

As preacher, organizer, publicist, author, pastor and friend, Silvester Horne did a work in his short life that in volume and quality made him one of the remarkable religious leaders of his age. And over and around everything that he did, touching it with enduring beauty, was the radiance of a pure, joyous and unselfish life.

Boston.

Contents

LECTURE I

THE SERVANT OF THE SPIRIT

LECTURE I

THE SERVANT OF THE SPIRIT

I MUST begin the honourable task which your kind confidence has assigned to me by a simple and heartfelt acknowledgment of this high privilege. You have asked me to attempt an undertaking which can never have been an easy one, and which becomes measurably more difficult as the long sequence of volumes occupies shelf after shelf of our libraries. There were as you know humane laws under the old Hebrew dispensation in favour of those who had to toil for small reward as gleaners of the meagre residuum of the harvest-field after the more favoured harvesters had filled their barns to overflowing with grain of the earlier reaping. So far as I can see my predecessors have had little compassion on posterity. They never beheld my pathetic figure laboriously garnering the slender ears

they had overlooked, and submitting them
for acceptance to a highly-critical market.

Nevertheless, if I cherish for my distinguished predecessors just a faint sentiment
of envy, I trust I am able at the same
time to perceive that they did not have all
the good fortune. We are gleaning on a
field where history is being made every year.
The passage of the generations enhances the
splendour of the retrospect, and, in propor-
tion, the magnificence of the prospect. You
have not invited me here to lecture on an
obsolete art. This is not a funeral oration.
The prophet is not on the point of being
bowed out of the modern world. The
progress of civilization may make some professions unnecessary. With the world-wide
triumph of the Prince of Peace I take it the
soldier will make his final salute to the
nations ; and I suppose even the lawyer may
find existence somewhat precarious. Some
of us look to see the enterprise at present
associated with the manufacture and sale of
injurious liquors and implements of war
diverted to more wholesome channels.

Some trades and professions, it is clear, will die out as the kingdom of God comes to its own. But for every voice that carries inspiration to its fellows ; for every soul that has some authentic word from the Eternal wherewith to guide and bless mankind, there will always be a welcome. No changes of the future can cancel the commission of the preacher. He does not hold that commission from any human society. He is the servant of the Spirit. He is not the creation of a state, or a municipality. Societies may organize and reorganize themselves as they will. They may make and unmake their officials. Some commonwealths have chosen to break with the tradition of kingship. Some have tried every form of military dictatorship and civil despotism ; they have experimented with oligarchies, autocracies, and aristocracies. At times they have tried every form of government in swift succession. Possibly it is a wise thing that we should not cast our forms of national life in so rigid a mould. But in any case nobody would be bold enough to predict that this or that office

in the commonwealth is final and permanent ;
and may not be modified if society so de-
cides. You remember Mr. William Watson's
fine lines :

" The seasons change, the winds they shift and veer ;
The grass of yesteryear
Is dead ; the birds depart, the groves decay ;
Empires dissolve, and peoples disappear :
Song passes not away.
Captains and conquerors leave a little dust
And Kings a dubious legend of their reign ;
The swords of Cæsar they are less than rust ;
The Poet doth remain."

Suppose Watson had said, the prophet
rather than the poet ? For the prophet is of
older and nobler lineage, and his order includes all the children of inspiration whether
they have kindled the soul of the world by
speech or song. And I repeat, as society cannot commission a man to be a poet, even so it
is beyond the authority of any state however
powerful to create the prophet ; aye, or to
make his message false or barren, no matter
how governors may growl, and throned in-
iquities fulminate. No human authority can

credit or discredit his words.   His credentials
are of superior authenticity.   Let me state
the position I propose to occupy in these
lectures once for all, and at its highest.   The
preacher, who is the messenger of God, is the
real master of society ; not elected by society
to be its ruler, but elect of God to form its
ideals and through them to guide and rule
its life.   Show me the man who, in the
midst of a community however secularized
in manners, can compel it to think with him,
can kindle its enthusiasm, revive its faith,
cleanse its passions, purify its ambitions, and
give steadfastness to its will, and I will show
you the real master of society, no matter
what party may nominally hold the reins of
government, no matter what figurehead
may occupy the ostensible place of authority.

Nor is the office of the preacher in the
smallest danger of lapsing for lack of
candidates.   Our embarrassment arises from
riches not from poverty.   To-day everybody
will preach to us and at us, whatever qualifications for the function they may have or

lack. Never was this old world sown so
thick with pulpits. Never was heard in it
such superabundance of gospels. Who
that has ever read a modern newspaper
will affirm again that the dogmatist is
dead! Creeds jostle one another in the
market-place and in the drawing-room ; and
their often harsh and hoarse prophets and
prophetesses announce salvation and denounce judgment quite in the orthodox
style. Hot-gospellers to-day are a prolific
race ; and some of the beliefs for which they
woo and win converts speak volumes for the
credulity of mankind.

It is astonishing what eagerness there is
in our time to enter into competition with
the conventional and orthodox pulpit, and to
usurp its functions in dealing with the big
human problems. Now it is the dramatist
who is not content until he has converted the
stage into a pulpit; now it is the journalist
seeking to charm the public ear with some
message that he believes to be vital to the
common well-being; now it is the Socialist
agitator, on his soap-box rostrum at the

street-corner, making capital out of the in-
consistencies and hypocrisies of society, quite
in the old prophet strain; now it is the
novelist marshalling the forces of experience
and imagination, and training all his guns
on some citadel of real or fancied wrong;
now it is the statesman converting the platform of political expediency into the pulpit
of eternal principle; now it is the poet, or
the prose essayist, setting our highest and
wisest dreams of good to music and lifting
up the eyes of fallible human nature to the
hills whence cometh its strength. It must
sometimes appear to us that humanity is a
long-suffering, much-lectured creature, and
that not we of the churches only but journal-
ists, artists, politicians, novelists, playwrights
conceive their fellow-men and women as sitting in pews, patient and defenseless, at the
mercy of every would-be exhorter who has
discovered that they are not so good as they
should be.

Thomas Carlyle in his day expressed pity
for humanity whose ears were thus besieged
by armies of strident voices, in consequence

of which he, Thomas, lifted up his voice and shouted louder than all the rest. I confess to you I enjoy a quiet smile whenever the pessimists suggest that the vocation of the preacher is in danger of becoming obsolete. But I agree that God's order of preaching friars is a far wealthier society than some of us have recognized. America to-day will not forget to blazon upon the roll of her great nineteenth century preachers of righteousness the name of Abraham Lincoln as well as of Henry Ward Beecher; and Englishmen who are justly proud of Robert Hall and Thomas Binney, Dale and Spurgeon, cannot forget to number also among her national prophets Thomas Carlyle, John Ruskin and John Bright.

And why not? It is no business of ours to belittle our calling. We hold no brief for any narrow and exclusive theory of preaching. Inspiration is not conditioned by a white tie or a Geneva gown. I am glad to have listened to truths as noble and as Christian on the floor of parliament as have ever been uttered under the dome of St. Paul's. The Gettysburg speech was the message of a prophet of

God, even if it was not divided into three
heads and an application.   No, we who call
ourselves preachers enjoy no monopoly of
the greatest of all arts, nor are we interested
in establishing one.   The spirit breatheth
where it listeth.   Nobody doubts that Amos
was of us, though so far as I know he did
not, as we say, preach regularly twice a Sunday.   Ploughmen and herdsmen, carpenters,
fishermen, tax-collectors and tent-makers, sons
of German miners, Huntingdonshire farmers,
and Kentucky backwoodsmen, each in his
time and order, have received the divine affla-
tus, and therewith, the spiritual and moral
leadership of mankind.

History it is true gives little space to this
aspect of the progress of the race.   Its canvas is crowded with uniforms, of kings
and warriors and courtiers.   The romance
which the historian sees and describes to us
is the romance symbolized by the banners,
the martial music, and all the seductive pageantry of war.   But the real romance of history is this romance of the preacher; the
sublime miracle of the God-intoxicated soul

with vision of an eternal Will, and sense of
an empire to which all continents, tongues,
races belong.   This man stands serene amid
the clash of arms, and the foolish braggadocio
of Force, asking only for the sword named
Truth, for the harness of righteousness, and
the spirit of peace.   This is the world's unconquerable and irresistible Hero.   All its
most enduring victories are his.   It is he
who year after year, and generation after
generation, in spite of rebuffs, defeats and
disappointments, has planted the banner of
the kingdom of justice, freedom and humanity on the conquered and dismantled fortresses
of oppression, selfishness and wrong.

Do not think I am in danger of departing
from the special object of these lectures if I
strike this note at the outset.   It will do us
all good to realize *the catholicity and magnificence of our order*.   It is well to realize
that for justification of our existence we can
make appeal to an universal instinct.   We
may well cherish our affinities.   Our kith
and kin is the mightiest family under God's
heavens.

" Shakespeare was of us ; Milton was for us ;
  Burns, Shelley were with us ; they watch from their
      graves."

Certainly, no man was ever elect of God's
spirit to be the mouthpiece of Christian
righteousness who did not thereby confess
himself one of us.   The word " Sermon " has
sometimes had an uninviting sound.   It has
not always been associated with the melting
of the mists, and the vision of the infinite
blue.   Sometimes it is to be feared that it has
made the mists more dense, impenetrable and
chill.   We are not so prejudiced as to deny
the fact.   But rightly understood mankind
lives and grows on great sermons ; and in no
other way.   Sublime thoughts, high and holy
conceptions of life and death and duty, lofty
interpretations of nature and experience, the
light that reveals God upon the scene, and
that dignifies and glorifies human nature
—here is the substance of those great
sermons that enter into men's souls and
make them sons of God, and brothers of
humanity.

Have any of us fathomed the depth of that

supreme saying of our Lord's that the real
life of man is by "every word that proceedeth
out of the mouth of God"?   Every word!
The science of biogenesis is as compre-
hensive as that.   The vital ingredients in
our spiritual nurture are as manifold as that.
Every word of God, in whatever language
or dialect of the mother tongue of Deity, is
endowed with this creative power.   No single
syllable of the Divine speech but has in it
life-bearing, life-bestowing qualities.   Even
the inorganic creation is a mute evangelist.
The God who uttered Himself in nature has
decreed that its dumb lips should have their
own peculiar eloquence.   There are sermons
in stones.   In the rocks beneath our feet lie
the hoarded histories of past millenniums.
They are like ancient cinematograph films
by means of which the marvellous procession
of extinct existences passes before our wondering eyes, and stirs our sluggish imagination.   Of course it is possible to watch the
drama but to miss the meaning.   But even
Charles Darwin tracing the amazing progress
of the universe, and linking up as he be-

lieved all sentient existences to their flower
and consummation in the life of man, confessed that "at times there came over him
with irresistible force the conviction that he
had seen the Father." Then again, as he
sadly confessed, he lost the vision.

But alas! there is nothing extraordinary
in that experience. Because we make every
use of Nature except to hearken to her sublimest message, it does not follow that she
has lost her soul, and discarded her prophet's
mantle. Only we are, as our fathers used to
say, *gospel-hardened* to her words of truth
and grace, and especially to their more secret
and subtle meanings. Some day she will
surprise us in a more sensitive and respon-
sive mood, and show us in her mirror the
very countenance of Deity, and we shall
know that the place we stand on is holy
ground. After all, Wordsworth's Peter Bell,
sordid and vulgar, is not altogether false to
the possibilities of life when he is represented
as overwhelmed by a sudden revelation of
Nature's inner glory; and the man to whom
before

" A primrose by the river's brim
A yellow primrose was to him
And it was nothing more,"

looks into the heart of Nature's handiwork,
hears a Voice commanding him to worship
and believe, and becomes from that hour a
changed man, awakened from moral and
spiritual torpor.

A primrose in God's hands is text enough
to shatter all our shallow agnosticisms, and
reward our honest quest for the Eternal.
"Whither can I go from Thy presence?"
cries the psalmist with his poignant sense of
the unescapable Preacher, who has freighted
every atom of an infinite universe with
Divine lessons, warnings, appeals and in-
spirations. "If I ascend into the heavens
Thou art there; if I descend into hell behold Thou art there." Above the earth, the
glittering heavens declare the glory of God ;
and beneath it the dark secrets of the under-
world cannot be explored without Him.
Somehow, you and I have been staged in an
infinite theatre, every fragment of which represents some letter in the Divine caligraphy,

some note or tone in the ineffable oratorio music, in which the spheres sing the arias; and yet not an electron, infinitely minute, but has its part in the chorus. That is how we conceive it. The Universe is itself a great Bible, with the sublimest of all intelligible themes to set forth and illustrate, and with its myriads of worlds so many chapters expanding the one central and vital revelation, until by endless iteration, recapitulation and accumulation of evidence, the argument is established on which immortal souls can build an unconquerable faith.

I do not forget that there are many to whom the whole creation is inarticulate, and the universe eloquent of Nothing. To them the final achievement of our humanity is unconsciousness of God. The progress of the race is marked by the gradual unlearning of the spiritual lore of its childhood. Slowly but surely, one by one, every prophet voice is to be silenced, without and within. The solemn call to the human soul to recognize its origin and its destiny in God is to be heard no more. The worlds resolve them-

selves into masses of matter, many of them
mere useless derelicts on the ocean of space.
They cease to be the flaming manuscripts of
the Eternal Wisdom, with their address to the
conscience and reason of mankind.   From this
green earth the dews of inspiration are withered ; the bloom of its higher mystic beauty
is fled.   It becomes merely a ball of ponder-
able matter revolving aimlessly in unfathom-
able space ; the chance grave of innumerable
generations of existence that once cherished
the pathetic illusion that underneath them
were Everlasting Arms.

The evolutionist, tracing the history of
man, finds this astonishing phenomenon,—
that once there dawned on man the consciousness of God, that the dawn ripened
into the perfect day, and then that the light
faded from the sky, and the human soul
passed through the twilight of dubiety into
the night of dark and sterile negation.   The
Universe will then become like some ruined
and dismantled abbey or cathedral, once aglow
with light and beauty, and, as it were, quiver-
ing with music, attesting its high **heroic**

human faith in God and man; but now
with altar desolate and prostrate pulpit, and
mouldering fabric, no longer a witness to the
world of spirit, no longer a trysting-place between the human and the divine, no longer
the sanctuary where the oracles of heaven
are heard and tested and believed. That is
what we are sometimes threatened with.
Men may conceive the universe as a vast
warehouse; but it will cease to be a church.

Over against such a possibility there is
the undeniable fact that every fragment of
creation is endowed with the preaching
office, and man with a soul that cannot be
insensitive to the universal appeal. Nor has
he proved himself to be so. From a thousand immortal canvases he has uttered and
still utters the truths with which Nature has
indoctrinated him. He has made himself
her expositor, her interpreter. Through him
she has expressed her inner meaning. And
not only by the artist's canvas but by the
language of the poet we are admitted to the
shrine where the *arcana* of Nature are communicated to us. The materialists who

flatter themselves that they are about to im-
poverish the universe of its idealism forget
that they have not only to fight down the
instinct of worship in every human breast,
but to make war against all the supreme
interpreters of Nature,—musicians, artists,
poets and the rest—who saw into the heart
of things with illuminated Vision, and dedicated their genius to proclaim what they
saw. The significant fact is that every man
is surrounded by the Voices that call to life ;
and that no one can ever be quite sure that
he has closed every avenue through which
divine appeals may reach his highest nature
and start new processes of faith which may
wholly change his character and his destiny

" Just when we're safest, there's a sunset-touch,
    A fancy from a flower-bell, some one's death,
    A chorus-ending from Euripides,
    And that's enough for fifty hopes and fears."

At any moment, in any place, we may find
ourselves in church, at worship. The heart,
so securely garrisoned, may be suddenly
stormed. Before we know it we have made

the fateful concession, and thereby signed our capitulation. God has taken a text, and preached. We can say with the young prophet of long ago, " The angel came and waked me, as a man is waked out of sleep."

In all of this there is no suggestion that the office and function of the preacher can ever be superseded. Rather he has his roots in the nature of things, and can never cease to fulfill his mission until all the works of God cease to be eloquent of the love and wisdom of their Creator. It may be true that of late years mankind generally has been tempted to lay the accent on other instrumentalities. The State bulks more largely in the thought of the average man to-day than the Church does. The statesman and politician are, in the thought of our democracies, clothed with almost limitless powers for the betterment of human conditions. They have a very attractive and absorbing gospel to preach. Their sermons are of higher wages, better houses, the fairer distribution of wealth, and the shortening of the hours of labour.

Their sphere of action is this present life, with its urgent immediate needs ; and just because their aim is avowedly to make this present world a better place to live in, they will never fail to find an audience.

You remember the sort of popular appeal that George Eliot put into the mouth of " Felix Holt, the Radical," when he took up his parable at the street corner against the churches and the parsons : " The aristocrats supply us with our religion like anything else and get a profit on it. They'll give us plenty of heaven. We may have *land* there. But we'll offer to change with them. We'll give them back some of their heaven, and take it out in something for us and for our children in this world." When things have gone wrong with us socially and industrially, preaching such as that makes many strings to vibrate in the average human breast. It is natural that the multitude should begin to fix their hopes on what governments can do for them, and should have but little patience with the evangelist who would hand to Lazarus, greedy for crumbs, a tract on the bliss he will enjoy when he gets to Abraham's bosom. God forbid that I should deny that there is a suggestion of irony in talking of the bread of life to the physically starving, the raiment of righteousness to those in threadbare rags, and the mansions of the blessed to those living in garrets or cellars. Most of us do not believe, any more than Felix Holt did, that the purpose of religion is to reconcile us to the postponement of all comfort and all luxury until we pass into another world. No sane critic will ever accuse the Lord Christ of being indifferent to the physical well-being of the people.

But readers of George Eliot's famous story will remember that Felix Holt's social ministry was the result of a moral and spiritual crisis to which he confessed ; and it had not occurred to him to enquire whence the impulse came prompting him to social service and political propagandism on behalf of the disinherited. " The angel came and waked me," said the young prophet Zechariah, and could give no clearer account. All he knew was that for years he had been in a state of

somnambulism—as one walking in his sleep.
He had lived for the superficial, for the things
of sense.   The things of the spirit had been
outside his consciousness.   Then came the
visitation—the influence of the higher ministry—and his soul awoke.   You are familiar
with Sant's popular picture of " The Soul's
Awakening."   The young girl has been reading in some book of vision ; and now she is
looking up with the aspect of one to whom
Revelation has come, and who has found
God and Life and Duty.   When Zechariah
was awaked, shaken out of sleep, and forced
to open his eyes upon reality, we are told
what it was that he saw.   A new civilization !
A city with streets in which the children
played, and where the inhabitants grew old ;
where there was work for all and leisure for
all.   A city, too, built without walls, unarmed, unfortified, with open gates hospitable
to all mankind, the symbol of peace and
brotherhood.

This is the vision of an awakened youth.
It is not unreal though it is as yet unrealized.
On the contrary, it is the kind of vision

which ought to be a permanent endowment
of every preacher's imagination. The one
thing needful to make us prophets is
an experience akin to that of Zechariah
—the soul's awakening. Some angel of
the Lord, some messenger from His Presence, some ministry of His Hands must
wake us out of our sleep. Of this I am
very sure—no preacher will thrill and move
his generation who has not himself known
this kindling of the soul. For it is "soul"
the world needs. Everywhere to-day I hear
the same complaint—that we are suffering
from lack of soul. Art, they tell us, shows
no falling off in skill of technique, but
there is so little soul in modern pictures.
Music is the same; the great composers have
left no successors. Poetry died out in the
nineteenth century. It is the same in other
spheres. The employer complains that his
workmen put no soul into their work. The
workman retorts that industries to-day are
managed for the most part by companies;
and companies are well enough called
"bodies" of men, but they are bodies with-

out souls. Even the pulpits of the world, I hear it said, are occupied by those who unite to a chaste style a well-furnished mind, and a genius for criticism and analysis; but somehow there is little soul, and the winds of heaven do not sweep over the spirits of their audience as in days gone by.

All this may be exaggerated. I suspect it is. But nobody can question that there is a measure of truth in it. And here, remember, is something that no parliaments or congresses can do. Here governments are impotent. If they could put money in every one's pocket, a good roof over every one's head, and the best clothes on every one's back; still they could not put a soul of faith and love in every one's breast. Here the preacher has really no competitor. There is something in the living voice of the true prophet that thrills us as nothing else can. We may be rich and increased with goods and yet have need of everything. Poverty is not the most fatal enemy of empires. The great empires of yesterday did not go to their ruin because of any lack of wealth.

They were on the contrary enervated by luxury. They perished, like Hamlet's father,
"full of bread." They declined and fell for
lack of " soul." Where there is no " vision "
the people perish. The appearance of a true
preacher is the greatest gift that any nation
can have. By his presence, and his spirit,
he multiplies the fighting forces for righteousness indefinitely. John Knox's voice was
as the sound of a trumpet. When Luther
rode to Worms, every timid believer in the
Reformation plucked up heart to speak and
act more boldly. When Cromwell arrived
on Marston Moor, the historian tells us that a
great shout went up in the Puritan camp
which was the presage of victory. It was
more. It *was* victory. What Washington
and Lincoln were to your own heroic fathers
in their day of trial, men of faith, men of
soul, men of God, are to all hard-pressed
Christian causes and all humane enterprises.
It is this force that we call " soul " that is
the motive-power of all progress ; that turns
all the wheels that ever *do* turn to any
noble purpose. " The words that I speak

unto you," said Jesus, "they are soul." **As** a mere matter of fact He has kept the soul of the world alive. As John Morley wrote many years ago, "The spiritual life of the West has burned during all these centuries with the pure flame first kindled by the sublime Mystic of the Galilæan Hills."

This is our business—the business which all the parliaments of the world are powerless to transact. I might have called the subject of these lectures, in which I hope to review some of the more notable preaching exploits of history, "Keeping the soul of the world alive." I have preferred to call it "The Romance of Preaching." Frankly, I fear that in these modern days we have been losing our sense of the splendid possibilities of our vocation. The thought of it does not thrill us. We do not go down to our work as we should, with our hearts beating high for the wonder and the hope of the adventures. We tend to become slaves to the routine of it. Once we were alive in the age of miracles. By "the vision splendid" we were "on our way attended." But the beauty

is off the morning sky, the glow of the dawn
is past. We have

> " seen it die away
> And fade into the light of common day."

There is no tragedy in all the world like
the disillusioned minister. He has to keep
on preaching. His congregation is often
weary ; but no one is so heavy of heart as he
is. "What a genius I was," cried Swift,
"when I wrote that book !" referring to a
work of his early prime. Millais, in the
presence of a collection of the pictures repre-
sentative of the splendid idealism of his
youth, burst into tears and rushed out of the
building. Somehow, so many of us are
strangers to the truth of Paul's affirmation
that "experience worketh Hope." So many
have gathered doubt and even despondency
as the fruit of that tree. So we begin to
envy other men their tasks. The physician
who with reverent hands and spirit repairs
the temple of the body ; the lawyer who
serves the ideals of justice ; the statesman
who helps to rear the fabric of a nation's

prosperity or a world's peace ; the explorer
and the engineer who between them prospect
and build the roads for a higher civilization
—all these we begin to believe are following
the gleam with nobler ambitions and to a
more glorious goal.

That, in part, is why youth does not rally
to the call of the ministry to-day, and why
the preacher's face is all too often in the
shadow.   The time has surely come to sound
another note.   Who should be proud of their
calling if not we?   What other history has
ever equalled ours?   Think of the procession
of the preachers!   No range of mountains
has been high enough to stay their progress ;
no rivers deep and broad enough to daunt
them ; no forests dark and dense enough to
withstand their advance.   No poet has ever
sung the epic of their sacrifices.   Was ever
such a romance ?   Was ever love exalted to
so pure a passion?   Was ever in the human
soul so unquenchable a fire ?   Silver and gold
they had none.   They did not seek to win
mankind by materialistic gifts.   Such as they
had they gave.   The alms they distributed

were faith, hope, love. Wherever they went they trod a pilgrim road, and flung forth their faith, often to a sceptical and scornful generation. But what heeded they? They passed onward from frontier to frontier, "the legion that never was counted," and, let us add, that never knew defeat.

Gradually before their message, ancient pagan empires tottered, heathen despots bowed the head, in the lands of Goth and Vandal stately cathedrals reared their splendid towers and spires, and the battle music of the Christian crusade rang triumphantly in chiming bells and pealing organs over conquered races. In the recesses of Indian forests, up the dark rivers of Africa and South America that often flowed red, along the frozen coast of Greenland and Labrador, the pioneer preachers made their pilgrimage. Let every village preacher who climbs into a rude rostrum, to give out a text and preach a sermon to a meagre handful of somewhat stolid hearers, remember to what majestic Fraternity he belongs, and what romantic traditions he inherits. He, too, is the servant of the spirit. He, too, does his work in the land of Romance. Many modern influences have tried to kill the consciousness of this truth. Even the churches do not always allow us to realize it. Materialism and rationalism would fain lay sacrilegious hands upon our task, and secularize it. But the true Prophet has that within his soul which no external adversaries can destroy.

> " I see my call ! It gleams ahead
> Like sunshine through a loophole shed !
> I know my Task ; these demons slain
> The sick earth shall grow sound again ;—
> Once let them to the grave be given,
> The fever-fumes of Earth shall fly !
> Up, Soul, array thee ! Sword from thigh !
> To battle for the heirs of Heaven ! "

LECTURE II

THE FIRST OF THE PROPHETS

LECTURE II

THE FIRST OF THE PROPHETS

THE Prophet stood in the old world as a mysterious and romantic figure, played upon by strange and sublime lights, his speech charged with subtle meanings, his life commissioned out of the supernatural for surprising and perilous errands. His is by far the most arresting figure in the Old Testament. When he takes the stage all other actors are dwarfed. If he is not there, time itself seems to wait for his appearance. Prince and priest alike are insignificant in his majestic presence. In his highest exemplars both his words and his deeds are memorable. His interventions, his appearances mark the crises of history. His words set the standard of thought for generations. With the people he is by no means always popular. He has no genius for smooth speech. He flatters neither monarch nor mob ; and nations have seldom loved the

uncompromising truth. He appears on the
canvas of Holy Writ as the clear-sighted
enemy of powerful, selfish, vested interests ;
and the passages are yet to be discovered in
which he pronounces blessing on the rich.
The language he holds is scathing and passionate ; and in many cases the denunciations
are more frequent than the consolations. Mr.
Matthew Arnold would perhaps have called
the prophet a Philistine ; but imagination
fails to conceive what the prophet would have
called Mr. Matthew Arnold.

But whatever be the type of mission and
of personality, the prophet dominates the life
of his time. Wherever and whenever he appears men's souls are stirred, and there is a
shaking of the dry bones. We realize that
he awes even the worldly-minded. He fixes
men's thoughts on serious issues. He rebukes
their triviality and flippancy. He brings a
breath of reality into ordinary conversation.
He confronts the careless and frivolous with
the claims of the Eternal. We realize, too,
that the great prophets had a genius for the
unexpected and the unconventional. They

ignored tradition. They were fiery iconoclasts, intolerant of illusions however fashionable. They had no excessive respect for the
orthodoxy so-called of the rigid schools of the
Rabbis. Of ceremonies and ordinances as
you know they were apt to speak with very
slight respect. The tendency of religion in
all ages to stereotype its forms and formulas
was viewed by the prophets as an insidious
evil. Thus it was never long before they had
arrayed against them all those who were
keenly interested in the preservation of the
old order of things. For the prophet was always and everywhere a reformer, zealous to
reconstruct life as it is so that it might more
perfectly express the will of God.

You will bear this in mind also, that even
when the people believed but little in their
prophet, the true prophet never faltered in his
belief in the people. He knew their souls
were soil adapted to the seed. He knew
that they were capable of all the aspirations
and all the heroisms which they habitually
professed to despise. He knew that their ag-
nosticism was superficial, and their contempt

of idealism a pose.   Let any genuine voice
reach them and thrill them, or let some great
crisis shatter their slumbers, and their affecta-
tions, and all the inferior creeds would go
down before the resistless tide of spiritual
feeling.   Unless there is in men and women
this capacity of re-birth the preacher's work
everywhere is vain ; we may as well dismantle
our pulpits, and recognize that human progress is a delusive hope.   So Thomas Carlyle
exclaims concerning the European Reformation : "Nations are benefited, I believe, for
ages by being thrown into divine white heat
in this manner, and no nation that has not
had such divine paroxysms at any time is apt
to come to much."   The preacher, it is true,
may feel himself to be, in the beginning, only
a voice crying in the wilderness, but he also
believes that the desert can rejoice and blossom as the rose.   That is to say, he believes
that actual desert is potential Eden ; and that
all that is needed to effect the miracle is the
coöperant forces of what we describe as the
Sun of Righteousness and the Water of
Life.

This inspired visionary, with his radiant belief in transfigured deserts,—in sandy and barren wastes gay with lilies and roses—is surely the very insuppressible hero of Romance. He walks the mean streets and dreary paths of modern industrial districts, with the same high confidence that lighted the face of Isaiah amid the desert of commercialized Judaism, in the unspiritual environment of ancient Babylon. For he believes in his people; he is sure of his audience. It is nothing to him that they do not believe in themselves. It is nothing to him that the soil to be cultivated is so heavy and obstinate a clay, or so barren a waste. The more unpromising the material, the more smiling is his prevision of success. This, surely, is the element of futurity about the prophet's message which has often been fiercely debated. He is more than a forth-teller. He *is* a fore-teller. He does "dip into the future." It is given to him to see the end from the beginning. More certainly than the scientist with boasted precision can dogmatize on the ultimate product in the total process of cause and effect, the prophet fore-

sees and foretells the inevitable transformations that will be produced upon the desert
of unbelief and unrighteousness, by the operation of the Divine Spirit.

But let us leave these generalizations and
make a more close and detailed study of
the first great master of the art of the prophet
as he is portrayed for us in the Book of Exodus.   To those who frankly disbelieve that
the message of God to man is even more than
the call to personal regeneration, and who
are aghast at the idea of the preacher being
made the instrument of popular liberty and
social reconstruction, the mission and message
of Moses must be the source of endless difficulty.   On what theory they rely for explain-
ing away this man and his work I have no
notion.   But to the candid student who holds
no brief for, or against, any particular theory,
the story of Moses is surely one of the most
luminous and thrilling in human history.

I need not dwell here on the romantic cir-
cumstances of his preservation from death,
and his transfer from the hovel of the slave
to the palace of the Pharaoh.   His education

is more to the point. Do not fail to note
that the Scripture assumes that it belonged
to the will and purpose of Providence that
this first great Hebrew prophet should be in-
structed in all the lore of the Egyptians.
There was no prejudice against what is
sometimes derided as pagan or classical culture. Familiarity with the thoughts and
imaginations of great men is taken as an invaluable preparation for the preacher's work,
even when these thinkers belong to a very
different school of religious philosophy.
Like the apostle Paul, his mental powers are
trained and disciplined in the wisdom of the
ancients, but his personality and his experience are his own ; and so far as we can see,
he is never in any danger of surrendering his
personality or depreciating his experience.

His nearest successor in modern times was
John Wesley whose whole preaching was
coloured by his classical learning, who
abounded in illustrations drawn from the
ancients, and yet the originality of whose
spiritual experience was the secret of his
unique influence over his generation. It can

never be necessary in this atmosphere to protest against any and every theory that makes
light of an educated ministry, and that assumes that Providence prefers to let loose
upon an unsophisticated generation the man
of undisciplined mind.   I shall have more to
say on this subject when I come to deal with
the Romance of Evangelism.   But for the
present let me lay it down that there is nothing in Holy Writ to warrant the assumption
that a man is likely to be more spiritual if he
is an ignoramus ; or that prophetic power in
the pulpit especially attaches to the preacher
whose heart is full and whose head is empty.
Knowledge is really not a disqualification for
the ministry ; neither is there any incompati-
bility between the seer and the scholar.   Because Festus chose to assume that much
learning had made Paul mad, we need not be
seriously afraid that a similar cause will be
likely to produce that effect in us.   That
Moses brought to his great democratic task
a finely trained, balanced and disciplined intellect was of immeasurable value to him, and
gave him at once a portion of personal as-

cendency when he came to deal with those whose misfortune it was, that they had been deprived of his advantages.

But on the most vital point of all, the Scripture narrative is emphatic. No weight of learning, no insight into alien creeds, and no increase of social prestige injured his humanity. In the court atmosphere that he breathed, and under the tuition of the Egyptian scholars, he did not lose his capacity for indignation, his passionate hatred of oppression and love of liberty. Neither did his own prosperity make him forgetful of those who were the victims of cruelty, and apparently in the grip of an inexorable fate. His eulogists were wont to celebrate the meekness and patience of his later days. But I do not think I am wrong in saying that in every true prophet there is something volcanic. Well is it for all of us when our primal instincts remain intact, however thoroughly we may master the lessons of self-control. Moses in his young manhood betrays the depths of his humanity—his elemental hatred of oppression ; but I ask you to observe that

when he fled from the consequences of his
own rough blow struck for justice and freedom, he is guided to a solitude where he
might think out his problem. For the problem was not only to avenge one wrong but
to destroy the system that authorized the
wrong. After all it was a poor thing merely
to strike down the agent of Pharaoh's tyranny. The war Moses had to wage was
against the throned iniquity, the entrenched
and panoplied injustice that had behind it all
the force of organized authority, and all the
glamour of a throne. In other words, the
problem for this Man of destiny was how to
end an iron despotism and substitute an
order of justice, freedom and humanity. No
preacher into whose soul God's light has
penetrated will ever content himself with
seeking the deliverance of the individual, so
long as systems of wrong are allowed to
stand which have issue, generation after generation, in the demoralization of human nature, and the consequent perpetuation of injustice.

The next stage in the ordeal of Moses may

be described as his fight against his destiny.
For it has always been true that God's best
ministers take up their commission under a
sense of compulsion. They cannot easily
believe that this awful and sublime call is to
them. They are conscious of no capacity in
their nature equal to so tremendous a vocation. They are driven out on to these great
waters, where the Divine business is to be
done, under stress of storm. It needs the
utter maximum of revelation to convince us
that we are actually the elect of God for tasks
so mighty. Like Moses, we plead nature's
bar, and cry "Impossible!" "O Lord, I am
not eloquent. . . . And the Lord said,
Who hath made man's mouth, is it not I the
Lord?" Science has laboured in our time to
make a Gospel out of natural selection. But
this Gospel of supernatural election is a
greater one. God's miracles are wrought by
those who, in spite of themselves, do the humanly impossible.

You remember a passage in one of Mr.
Augustine Birrell's essays in which he reminds us that the poet Gray longed to be a

soldier ; he wrote the immortal elegy but he took no Quebec ; General Wolfe took Quebec, and with his latest breath declared he would rather have written Gray's elegy.   Not natural selection, but divine election !   Frederick William Robertson broke his heart because he might not be a soldier ; and was constrained into the office of prophet by influences he could not comprehend.   Yet, so coerced in spirit, he preached ; and did more than any other of his time to create a new birth of faith.   Not natural selection but supernatural election.   Strange as it seems, and paradoxical, God's noblest warriors have felt like pressed men.   Said a young fellow once before a college committee when asked why he wanted to enter the ministry, " Because all other ambitions went down before the revelation of life in Christ."   The other ambitions *have* to go down.   The one and only ambition that is big enough to overwhelm all others has to master and possess the preacher.   I know nothing in history more impressive than the resistless way in which God urges His claims ; how He seems to shut in the man to the task, and sweep away his objections and hesitations like chaff before the wind.

> " So nigh is grandeur to the dust,
>   So near is God to man,
>   When Duty whispers low, 'Thou must,'
>   The soul replies, 'I can.'"

It is that determinative " thou must " that lies behind the consecrated audacity of the prophet, and lends strange fire to his words.

Surely there is no prayer more appropriate to any one who feels the inner urging of the spirit towards the office of the preacher than the famous one of Augustine—" O God, give what Thou commandest and then command what Thou wilt." When we are ready to cry out with Moses, " I cannot go, I have not the gift, I should only bring dishonour upon the cause," the answer is, " The gift is in the good pleasure of the Giver." Certain it is He will send no man on any errand of His, without the ability to discharge it.

Yet this diffidence on the threshold is surely

a sign of grace. We notice it not only in Moses but in Jeremiah, in Zechariah and in Paul. They require to be convinced that they are not being tempted to build the most responsible and difficult of all lives on mere raw impulse. They are resolved to hold no illusions as to their own character and capacity. They weigh, and measure up, their powers and talents with scrupulous exactitude. They disguise none of their deficiencies. They do full justice to the magnitude of the work required of them. Then with genuine humility they object their insufficiency for the task. Only men who have approached the ministry in this spirit have had their souls and wills purged from the alloy of false and base ambitions. But at the last, Moses is made to see that his mistrust of self and his fear of failure, alike spring from an imperfect knowledge of God and partial surrender to His will. The one thing lacking in the special education of Moses for the crisis in history which he has to handle is Revelation. The solution of Israel's social problem lies precisely where the solutions of

all social troubles lie,—in the knowledge of
God and of His will.

It is this experience to which the next
chapter in his education is sacred. The
special gift that is to fit him for his ambas-
sadorship is God's revealed secret to him—a
new knowledge of God which former generations had not known, nor needed to know, but
which was revealed to him, Moses, because
without it he could not accomplish his task.
It is well to take note of the actual words as
they are given us in the Book of the Exodus.
The passages are gathered from two chapters.
To the petition of Moses for new light on the
nature of God the answer is, "I AM hath sent
thee"; and it dawns on this young Liberator
that this mystic message contains a new truth
of pregnant meaning—"I am the Lord; I
appeared unto Abraham, Isaac and Jacob by
the name of God Almighty but by my name
JEHOVAH was I not known to them." This
spiritual crisis in the personal preparation of
the prophet for his work is worthy of your
attention. By some flash of inner light he is
conscious of out distancing the greatest of

his predecessors. Some new conviction is burned into his brain. He is literally on fire with a new ideal.

"O glory of the lighted mind,"

exclaims Mr. Masefield's converted hero in "The Everlasting Mercy." There is no glory equal to it. In that hour Moses became a seer, and stands illuminated with the glory of the lighted mind.

In the first place it is a great thing to know by actual verification that *Revelation is progressive.*

"Each generation learned
    Some new word of that great Credo which in
        prophet hearts has burned
    Since the first man stood God-conquered with his
        face to Heaven upturned."

It is one thing to believe that as a theological proposition ; it is quite another thing to know its truth in some hour of exalted vision. This is the very soul of religion. It thrills us in those majestic words which form the stately exordium of the Epistle to the Hebrews,

" God who at sundry times and in divers manners spake in time past unto the fathers by the prophets hath in these latter days spoken unto us by His Son." " God hath spoken." This is the life of truth. God hath spoken to *us*. The Divine word has become cogent and pertinent to our life and our need. Something of the infinite reserve of truth has been specially disclosed for our enlightenment. We are not the disciples of a closed canon. Do not the astronomers tell us that we live in so splendid and spacious a physical universe that not a year passes but the light from some new star, some effluence out of the Infinite, reaches our world and adds to our perception of the wealth of the Eternal ? And are we to suppose that the spiritual universe is less august ? and that those rays that speak of realities old as the worlds yet new to our ken, may not reach our souls to-day, and continue to illumine with fresh radiance the spirits of the generations yet unborn ? We are the heirs of progressive revelation. We are admitted to know secrets withheld from the knowledge of our

sainted sires.   We are always knowing God.
To know Him is the life which is life indeed.

The special revelation that lighted the
mind of Moses and made him a prophet lay in
the name of God—the I AM, the Eternal Presence ; or as Dr. Fairbairn more truly phrases
it, "He who causes to be."   This is the
Vision of the Immanent Deity without whom
there is no existence and no progress ; and
who has not made either the world or humanity but is ever making them.   This is the
Vision of the Will that rolls through all
things, moulding and making all that is.
The soul that is one with that Will is lifted
above fear and failure.   For him the Present
is alive with God ; and the Future is forever
with Him.   That is the faith with which to
conquer the hell of slavery ; that is the vision
to give hope and patience to the Reformer
whose business it is not only to deliver the
people's bodies from bondage but their souls
from the curse of captivity.   "*I Am* hath
sent thee."   It is not very far from that
revelation to the central Christian faith—
Emmanuel, God with us.

Here then is our man, the first in the august line of the prophetical succession, one who of his own choice espouses the cause of a suffering people, who for the sake of the enslaved and oppressed eats the bread of exile and servitude, who by Divine constraint takes up the sacred but thankless task of liberator, and becomes the mouthpiece of the will of God alike to tyrant monarch and depraved multitude. He is the servant and spokesman of " Him who causes to be." On that revelation of the Divine purpose and co-operation he relies, and under the inspiration of it he rises to a sublime height. He sees that the social revolution without which national emancipation cannot be achieved lies within the will and power of Him who causes to be. Henceforth Moses is a " God-intoxicated " man. But so far from being a visionary, his spiritual illumination confers practical insight and the wisdom of statesmanship. He has not only to persuade a dark, degraded and discouraged people that their social misery is not irremediable nor their spiritual despair indestructible if only faith in God revives in their breasts ; but he has somehow to lead them up from the depths of servitude and fashion for them a religious and social system which shall incorporate and express the new revelation of God and His will.

I need not tell you that our inspired prophet was no infallible pope. As we have seen he was the disciple of progressive revelation, and just as he saw truths about God that had been concealed from his fathers, so the generations to come would outgrow the Mosaic system in the light of a still purer and humaner revelation. Something of the harshness and inhumanity of the heathenism from which his race had emerged betrays itself in many of his statutes. But it is not the man's limitations that astonish us, but his almost incredible height of wisdom and humanity, standing where he did. And one supreme conviction masters him. God must rule the whole life of man. Nothing that is human must ever lie outside the divine governance. That is why he brings the will of God to bear on the minutest details not only of worship, but of conduct.

The wonder of the Mosaic legislation is not in the provision of the tabernacle and the elaborate system of symbol by means of which he designed to teach a people of very rudimentary religious education the spiritual and moral truths he himself had grasped ; the wonder of the Mosaic legislation is in the new social and economic order that it created, and the moral code that was to hold therein.   First, in the Decalogue, he not only sweeps away by solemn enactment all polytheism and idolatry, but all external temptations thereto.   Then he provides by law for one day's rest in seven for everybody. Then he lends the sanction of religion to that respect due to parents which is the key to a wholesome family life.   Then he legis- lates against murder, adultery, theft and scandal, and even ventures to lay the divine law upon the thoughts and imaginations of the heart by a statute against those envious desires which are the source of so many deeds of unjust aggrandizement.

So much for the Decalogue.   But there follows, as you know, the most elaborate and interesting series of statutes, dealing with various classes of labour, menservants and maidservants, for whom a whole charter of rights, exemptions and privileges is devised. He faces problems as to the responsibility of those who are the unwitting cause of injury to others. He is rigorous against usury. He safeguards the position of the "foreigner," and enjoins hospitality. He deals with the appointment of judges and decrees the punishment for perjury. He sketches the system of land tenure and asserts the original and inalienable proprietorship of God. He has a good deal to say as to the conduct of war, and while his words are in places dark and fearful, we have nevertheless in his statute the first attempt ever made to humanize war and moderate some of its consequences. His agrarian legislation includes details as to the cultivation of vineyards, and methods of ploughing. He even condescends to the character and quality of clothing that is appropriate to the life of the people; and again and again he throws the shelter of Divine authority about the life and

fortune of the poor, the infirm and the
"stranger"; as well as around the dumb
beasts that are the servants of mankind.

Perhaps I may be allowed to interpolate
here that my argument is scarcely, if at all,
affected by the most advanced criticism,
assigning much that has been included in
the code of Moses to a later date. It is really
a question of the foundation tradition of a
great people. The prophet comes upon the
scene as the herald of a theocracy. His soul
is alive with faith in the kingdom of God.
He sees that government by God's will means
not only the acceptance of certain beliefs, and
the performance of certain acts of worship,
but the observance of certain ethical obliga-
tions, and the organization of a certain social
order. The tradition of the Hebrew nation
was, from henceforth, that its state was
founded by its first prophet; that its first
statesman and legislator was one who received his ideals in communion with God
upon the Mount of Vision. No one can wonder that the successors of Moses in the great
prophetical line were similarly endowed by

the spirit for momentous political errands. Hence Samuel crowns and discrowns kings. Elijah, flying from life and duty to Horeb, hears commanding words bidding him return to the thick of the human fray "and anoint Hazael to be king over Syria and Jehu the son of Nimshi to be king over Israel." So he, too, becomes the instrument of political revolution, and the mouthpiece of the creed that the Lord God cares how the people are governed, and that His sovereignty remains unaffected by the particular mode of government that may obtain at any time and in any land. This then is the conception alike of the work of the preacher, and of the ideal constitution of a people that we derive from the Old Testament ; and as I hope to be able to show you in later lectures, it is not modified by any teaching or practice that we owe to the New Testament. The whole problem of good government is how to give effect to the ideal of the kingdom of God. The problem of bad government lies in the men who have lost sight of that ideal.

I think we may spare a few more thoughts
for the problem of how God made His first
great prophet—the leader of that hero race
whose deeds and words belong to the unper-
ishable glories of the world. You and I
come to our consideration of this man with
questions in our minds which we shall have
to answer, and in regard to which people will
look to us for guidance. Yet these questions
only differ in degree from those that tortured
the soul of Moses and inspired his sacrifice
and devotion. He became the man he was
because he saw the two extremes of life, its
luxury and its misery, its cruel indefensible
inequalities. I sometimes think no man is
qualified to be a preacher at all into whose
soul that iron has not entered. We may
state our economic beliefs to-day in more
scientific terms than Moses could. But do
we feel as much as he did what the actual
facts mean ? Do we realize the poignancy of
the contrast ? It was the great advantage of
this embryo prophet that he lived in both
worlds ; he knew the *want* at one end of the
social scale and the *waste* at the other. He

saw that the pomp and splendour of the court of the Pharaohs was all sweated out of the unpaid labour of the toilers. He saw the inside organization of a vast tyranny which kept multitudes in poverty that a few might revel in luxury and idleness. He saw the scorn and contempt of the exploiters of industrialism for those on whose labour they lived. He saw all these things; and according to a modern pietistic school, he would have done his duty if he had simply preached the existence of God, and had taken no step to break up this iniquitous order and give freedom and justice to the people. Fortunately for the Israelites he did not read his destiny and duty so.

It is no business of mine to suggest what subjects should be included in the curriculum of a college where men are in training to be preachers. The day will come, I suspect, when a course of instruction on social conditions will be a part of the normal education of every minister of religion. But desirable and important as that is, you cannot nourish the spirit and passion of a Moses simply on a diet of political economy and social statistics. What counts is actual experience of the cruelties and miseries of an organized society where unbridled prodigality at the top, is balanced by indescribable poverty at the bottom. The course of study I would fain include in the curriculum of every modern school of the prophets would be conducted in a tenement district, or some area where men and women live—or exist—doing unending tasks for starvation wages. If to that could be added a brief course of study of the actual lives of the wealthy dilettantists and neurotics who make up so large a portion of what is called Society, we should breed a race of prophets who would be our leaders in a new exodus towards a new land of promise.

When the great masses of our peoples are made to understand that our preachers are those who know the inwardness of their life and lot, and have entered into close brotherhood with them to champion their right to fullness of life and opportunity, then faith will revive in our lands even as we read in the time of Moses, " And the people believed, for when they saw that the Lord had visited His children, and had seen their afflictions, then they bowed their heads and worshipped."

Somewhere in your literature I have read the story of a scene after one of the battles of your Civil War. The rude hospital was crowded and the surgeons were busy with their instruments of pain. And in the midst of all the anguish and agony there stood a fair young girl who had devoted herself to the task of nursing. The turn of one of the wounded men had come, and his operation had to be faced. He said he thought he could bear it if the lady would come and hold his hand. And she went where he lay, and held his hand; watched the cold beads stand out on his brow; and gathered up into her heart all his suffering and pain. If the world bears its sorrow and miseries to-day with some measure of faith and fortitude it is because the Lord Christ has stood, during these centuries, by the bedside of a suffering Humanity and held its hand, and gathered into His Divine heart its pain, its grief, and its sin.

Remember, there is no cheaper way than this to bring about a revival of faith. Faith is often crushed out of the hearts of people by harsh and unjust social conditions. It is not unnatural that the victims of these conditions should argue from man's inhumanity to man either that the God who permits it is indifferent, or that there is no God since He does not intervene. It is little use to go to such as these and preach the theory of religion. Theology is a fascinating subject, but the formula has yet to be invented that will satisfy the souls of those who are suffering under the cruel lash of injustice, and who are the prisoners of circumstance. Some one must go to them who by his own life of brotherhood and practical sympathy will interpret to them God's redeeming purposes. Some one must do what Moses did for the Israelites—consecrate his sympathy, his sagacity, and his energy to the task of deliverance, and the substitution of the right for the wrong, which is the eternal world-task at which all must labour.

The Old Testament introduces us broadly

to two orders of preachers. Of the one
Elijah is the type — the uncompromising
individualist, remote, inaccessible, ascetic.
Ever and anon he descends from his solitudes to thunder his denunciations against an
apostate age. But he knows little of the
people, or of the time. He is apt to exag-
gerate his loneliness in righteousness. He
thinks the whole land has gone after Baal
while all the time there are seven thousand
non-conformists. But his courage, and his
austerity make him a power. The people
gaze with awe upon his face, even though
they look with relief upon his back. This is
a great type of preacher; but I question
whether it is the type that is most welcome,
or most potent. Elijah was succeeded by
Elisha; and the young disciple who received
for endowment a double portion of the old
preacher's spirit dedicated himself to a
totally different type of ministry. He was a
homely, friendly man, whose place was in the
hearts and homes of the people.

Think of the facts about him as we know
them. The Shunammite woman knew him

as the one man in the land who would understand what the loss of her lad meant to her.
The young prophets, eager to erect their
new house, put their arms around him, and
said, " Be content, and go with us." If they
had acted like that to Elijah, I do not know
which would have been the more uncomfortable party, the old prophet or the young
probationers. When the widow of a young
preacher comes to Elisha, he reads her
tragedy in shrewd human fashion. " What
hast thou in the house?" he asks, and she
answers pathetically, " Thine handmaid hath
not anything in the house, save a pot of oil."
When the Shunammite woman returned after
the famine to find her lands alienated, he
made himself at once her champion, and
faced the king with the demand, " Restore to
her her lands, and the fruits since the day she
left." This is the new order of ministry.
It is human, social, sympathetic. Elisha
knows how people live, enters into their
joys, shares their ambitions, instinctively dis-
cerns their privations, and will not see them
defrauded of their rights. Both orders of

ministry may have their place; but I believe
that the future will largely be the inheritance
of the latter. We are returning in thought
and feeling in these latter days to the ideal
which lies behind the Book of the Exodus,
and which is reflected in the renunciation,
the practical sympathy, the strenuous and
sagacious leadership, and the code of moral
and social legislation, of the first of the
Prophets.

LECTURE III

THE APOSTOLIC AGE

LECTURE III

THE APOSTOLIC AGE

THE great succession of the Hebrew prophets came to its conclusion and consummation in John the Baptist. He was of the school of Elijah. He practiced rigorous austerities. By his mode of life he evidenced the contempt in which he held the fashionable habits and ambitions of the day. The simplicities and severities of his existence harmonized well with the type of ministry to which he knew himself elect. It might appear from the substance of his preaching that he knew more of the necessity for repentance and reform than of the secret of regeneration. But however that may be he had no new vision of God ; and his greatness lay in the sublime humility with which he pointed the people away from himself to One who had the new Gospel that was to regenerate humanity and change the world. Yet John's preaching when he descended from the mountain solitudes to the fords of Jordan is worthy of your study. He was one of those fearless and clear-sighted souls who by his own utter sincerity, spiritual discipline and sacrificial life, had earned the right to strip society of its shams, expose and denounce its sins, and generally become its conscience in a way that only the most absolutely disinterested and single-minded men can ever dare to do.

I have said there was nothing exactly new in his ministry. His call to repentance was as old as the race. The spirit and forms of asceticism were not rare among his predecessors. His indifference to the materialistic aims on which most men's hearts were set was a genuine note of prophethood, but by no means unique. John's significance lies first of all in his sense of the nearness of the Messianic kingdom for which the ages had been in travail; and secondly, I think, in a very deep and true view of the social evils which had sprung from the corruption of religion. His first movement is to fling down a challenge to the ecclesiastical leaders because they had imbibed the worst vices of a self-constituted aristocracy. The senseless pride in blood and lineage, the perilous illusion, " We have Abraham for our father," had blinded them to reality and wrought their spiritual ruin. John's sane soul recognized the fatal error and folly which have so often been used to buttress up vast and illusive claims whether of ancestral descent or spiritual succession ; and with the courage and frankness of the true preacher he smote his sword through this web of lies. "God is able of these stones to raise up children unto Abraham," he cried ; and with that sharp final epigram, the whole baseless fabric of an artificial spiritual aristocracy crumbled to the dust.

Then he turned to the mixed multitude, who were asking to be shown their way of life, with a command which proved him as resolute to teach equality to them as to the religious magnates whom he had just humbled. "He that hath two coats let him impart to him that hath none," he cried, and left them to digest that unwelcome counsel of socialism as best they could. The revenue-raisers came next, and the Word of God in the person of John was heard for the first time in the New Testament in denunciation of " graft." This thunderbolt was followed swiftly by another when he flamed out against the military oppression and coercion which in Palestine was only typical of the age-long crucifixion of Right at the hands of Might. With a final affirmation that to end this reign of Wrong, and establish the Kingdom of Righteousness, One mightier than he was needed, and was on the way, John ended one of the shortest and most scathing sermons of which there is any record. On that mighty canvas of history where the figure of the Preacher is incomparably the most romantic of all, is there any more heroic and pathetic personality than this son of the desert with his ascetic frame and soul of fire, bringing his ministry to a consummation in a sublime act of self-effacement, and with courage unquenched turning his back on all scenes of popularity, and setting his face like a flint to a dungeon and a scaffold ?

I am now to invite you to concentrate your thought on the amazing era of apostolic preaching which followed the death and resurrection of our Lord, and of which the new vision of God that broke over the souls of the first disciples was the creative cause. It is common ground among the historians that this which we call the apostolic age is the Romance of all history. The story is of a dozen inspired workmen, who were lifted by an ineffable experience out of the deepest depths of humiliation and shame to serene heights of faith, whence they went forth to write the incomparable epic of world-conquest. There are no words in any language that can express how dear they held their faith and how cheap they held their lives. In all the instrumentalities on which we too often rely to win our victories they took no stock. They knew nothing of art, architecture, or music, nor for the most part did they reck much of education. They met the mailed hand of Rome unarmed and defenseless. With no material weapon, no organized army, no display of force, they shook the

mightiest of world empires till it trembled and
tottered.   From the handful of recreant
apostles who in the crisis of His fate had
failed their Leader, sprang the invincible
legion that did not know the meaning of
fear, and that, to use the words of one of our
own Puritan fathers in exile, " triumphed
over cruelty with courage, over persecution
with patience and over death itself by dying."
Rome had conquered every race, and tram-
pled upon every creed only to be baffled by
men whose bodies she could burn but whose
hate she could not provoke ; nay, whose love
she could not alienate.   When the sand of the
Colosseum was red with their blood ; when
in Nero's gardens, converted into torches, they
passed through smoke and flame to their rest,
their message swept in triumph from convert
to convert; while in the subterranean seclu-
sion of the catacombs the martyr missionaries
preached and prayed and signed the galleries
of Death with the symbols of eternal Hope.

But before I come to some illustrations of
this heroic age, there is a preliminary question to which I must attempt an answer.

Let me ask what was the new Revelation that fired men's souls with such sublime faith and fortitude? What was the new music that was to enchant its disciples and render them insensitive to torture and death? What was it that came to them through the Cross of Christ, and possessed them with a spiritual passion to which all history provides no parallel? For at Pentecost not only was faith born in the hearts of doubters, and courage in the hearts of cowards, but the passion for preaching was born in them all. "They *all* spake with tongues, and prophesied." Every one had a vision to describe, an experience to relate, a secret to tell. "All the Lord's servants were prophets." Something had been kindled within them that the terrors of Jerusalem could not chill. What was the new consciousness, the new conviction, that exalted them and made men and women of crudest speech eloquent? What was it that woke the slumbering poet in these simple natures, and charged their homely utterance with a power that the rhetoricians might well have envied? No doubt it is difficult, it may even seem presumptuous, to analyze their emotions. But we have the records to help us. We can trace the leading ideas that found expression in the first Christian sermons and the earliest Christian literature. We know what Peter taught, what Stephen testified, what Paul elaborated. We can read the challenge flung down to ancient creeds and civilizations. May I submit to you that the great new doctrines that received their inspiration and confirmation from Christ, and that became the very substance of the new Evangel, and the secret of its spiritual and social power, were two— *Immortality* and *Equality ?* There, if you come to think of it, are the two supreme gifts of our religion—*Life* and *Love.*

(1) That Christ's gift of life was more than the assurance of immortality we are all agreed. To do the Christians of that first century justice it was Christ they valued; and they would rather have been mortal with Christ than immortal without Him. But the fact remains that the theme of the first Christian preachers was the Resurrection and all its

consequences. Life suddenly revealed itself to them in a glory that took their breath away and smote them to their knees in awe and rapture. For they knew themselves now as "immortals," and the splendour of the destiny humbled and exalted them. You remember the famous king who appointed a man to say ever to him, "Philip, thou art mortal" lest an unworthy pride should be his undoing. But henceforth the pilgrim church was to whisper in the ear of Humanity, "Man, thou art immortal; live as one of the immortals, and may a noble pride in thy origin and thy destiny save thee from baseness and dishonour."

It has become a favourite criticism of the Christian fathers that, overwhelmed by the vision of eternal life in Christ, they became other-worldly and counted life here of little moment if only they could make sure of bliss hereafter. For my part I could wish that every modern Christian had passed even an hour under the stress of the emotion which a realization of immortality ought to bring to each human soul. You have to conceive,

not a solitary prophet like Paul, but a very
host of triumphant evangelists chanting the
ecstatic challenge, "O Death, where is thy
sting? O Grave, where is thy victory?"
What Egyptian and Jew had timidly and
darkly received, and to which Greek Philosophy had occasionally uttered a pale and
bloodless "perhaps," became to these witnesses the certainty of certainties, the truth
of truths. History has to recognize that
whatever did, or did not, happen on that first
Easter morning, at that "lone Syrian grave,"
the effect was to shatter the incredulity and
uncertainty of centuries, and out of dark
abysses of speculation drag life and immortality to light, and set man henceforth to fulfill his earthly destiny conscious of an unconquerable and indestructible soul. Whether
it is conceivable that that result was produced
by an illusion, and was the fruit of falsehood,
every one of us must judge for himself.
When I see similar far-reaching effects of
greatness spring from fallacy I shall myself
believe the illusion theory, and not till then.

The picture that we owe to St. Luke of the

early Church is of men and women living in the rapture of a great beatitude. They are illuminated with " the glory of the lighted mind." If you come to think of it, the Resurrection of Christ meant everything to them. It was the vindication of that Fatherhood of God which must have suffered eclipse in the seeming tragedy of Calvary ; it was equally the Divine vindication of Jesus, and the seal set upon His teaching and His life ; it was moreover the vindication of the greatness of the human soul and its amazing destiny. When you add to these the conscious leadership of the living Christ, and the creative power of the sublime faith *Ubi Christus ibi Ecclesia*, you begin to understand the light that transfigured the Christian people of Jerusalem, and transformed one obscure upper room into the very Gate of Heaven. If we were not so slow and hard of heart to-day we should still feel the uplift of this magnificent revelation ; we should still look upwards with the transports of the first Christians, and outwards with their reverence for humanity and faith in its future.

I confess to you I sometimes wonder
whether our hearts are big enough and brave
enough to attempt the Christian enterprise;
whether something of the world's morbid
and sceptic spirit has not darkened our sanctuary and paralyzed our very souls. Is it
not true that our ark lies prostrate in the
temple of Dagon instead of humbling to the
dust the pagan and heathen conceptions
against which we are professedly at war?
We have the most exquisite instrument
wherewith to discourse the most melting and
ravishing of music; but we play our Stradi-
varius with a mute. We are afraid of its full
tones. We fall back on the language of
Tennyson and count it a great thing if we
can say

> " We stretch *lame hands* of faith,"

or

> " We *faintly trust* the larger hope."

Lame hands and faint trust! With these we
think to win the victories that are only possible to the heroes of religion. Little wonder
that as the perplexed people listen on the one
hand to the arrogant dogmatism of material-

istic science and on the other to the halting and
hesitating and semi-apologetic discourse of
the modern prophet of religion, we make but
a poor appearance in the competition.

I do not want you to misunderstand me.
It may be that the preacher of open and sincere mind has been wrestling by the ford
Jabbok with the Angel of Truth and has
halted on his thigh. He is conscious that
somehow he walks lame in the paths his
fathers trod with sure steps and upright car-
riage. It may be that if we knew all, we
should take it for distinction; but the
preacher himself is only conscious that the
world has observed that he is lame, and is
asking if not where is thy God, at least where
is thy theology? And, believe me, we can
do nothing without the sublime simplicities
of Christianity. If a man does not know of
a surety that personal God whom even the
Prodigal at his husks can still speak of as
" *My* Father," if he cannot kneel by the sin-
stricken and announce to him with unclouded
faith the certainty of forgiveness in Christ, if
he cannot stand by the bedside of the dying

and encourage him in the sure and certain hope of the resurrection to eternal life, he may still do for the study, or the store, or the country house, but the Christian pulpit should know him no more.

I make even that last admission with some hesitation. For if we are in earnest in this matter we are bound to believe that this great creed is so determinative of character and life that no man—whatsoever his calling in life—can do his best work without it, and that apart from it every man's attitude to his fellows must be defective. Let me call to my aid a very brilliant leader of the medical profession in my own country. Addressing a meeting of medical students in the city of Sheffield, Sir James Crichton Browne advised them to beware of the materialistic school which regards a man's brain as no more than so much phosphorus and so much glue ; and suggested that if a man is good and wise it is because his brain has a maximum of phosphorus and a minimum of glue, while if he is evil and foolish it is because his brain has a maximum of glue and a minimum of phosphorus. Sir James went on to say that if the students adopted this materialistic conception of man's nature they would be disqualified from treating any one successfully as a patient even on the physical side. To be a true physician a doctor must understand the spiritual nature of his patients. The merely materialistic theory spells failure here and everywhere.

The best type of labour leader in my own land knows perfectly well how much is at stake in this great issue as to whether man is merely an animal of a higher order, and no more ; or whether he is, as Christ taught, an immortal being. If our workmen listen to the materialism that is preached to them from a thousand platforms and in a thousand journals, they lose the most powerful of all motives for social betterment. If they think and talk of one another as no more than animals they only have themselves to thank if employers treat them as if they were no more than animals. We, on the other hand, who believe with Christ in the nobility and dignity of human nature, must press upon the conscience of the community such questions as these. If the children of poverty and vice in the slums and alleys of our crowded cities, in cellars and garrets of tenement houses and elsewhere, are indeed immortal spirits destined to eternal existence, what is our duty to them? How can we sit with folded hands while men and women are wallowing in filth and slime who are sons and daughters of the Eternal? What new ideals of society are forced upon us when we dare to look at human life in the light of the Resurrection? In other words—what must our practice be, if we are still resolved to preach this magnificent Gospel?

(2) To the effect which the Evangelists of the Resurrection produced by their Gospel justice has been done by many historians. The violent antipathy of the Sadducaic school, which is always with us, manifested itself in an astonishing desire to exterminate all teachers who affirmed man's immortality. The heroic constancy of the Christian confessors in treating Death as no more than an

incident in Life, while it impressed the be-
holders, made the last dread weapon of the
persecuter of none effect; and so paralyzed
his arm. Of all this much has been written
again and again. But I think less justice
has been done to the effect of that new doctrine of Equality which found expression in
the organized life of the first Christian communities, and was a definite challenge to
every other social structure of the then
world. The principle running through these
primitive Christian societies was so simple
that it is difficult to realize how profoundly
revolutionary it was, and how subversive of
the existing order of things. But any one
can see that a church that offered equal
privileges to, and conferred equal rights
upon, the slave and the freeman; and acknowledged no authority of rank or station
within its borders, but reverenced faith and
character alone, threw down the gauntlet of
defiance to the most deep-seated prejudices
of our human nature.

Many a proud heart must have been the
theatre of a life-and-death struggle between

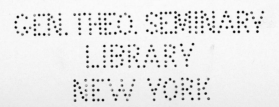

hereditary scorn of the "canaille" and a consciousness of the truth of the new Religion—such a struggle as Bulwer Lytton portrayed in the patrician breast of Glaucus in "The Last Days of Pompeii." One realizes that it was far less a matter of embracing the Christian doctrine than of accepting the Christian society that antagonized the aristocrats of Greece and Rome. When the waves of an invading and resistless Christianity flowed inward to the Imperial Throne itself, the terror it inspired was due, not so much to any of its distinctive dogmas, as to this amazing fraternity, the unity of which no extremity of coercion could injure or destroy. You are to imagine men and women, with a new and evident inspiration upon them, preaching this uncompromising truth that God holds all human souls at equal value, and thinks no more of a Constantine than of the humblest day-labourer whom he has treated as dirt beneath his feet.

No doubt it was strong meat, difficult of digestion at any time and in any place, but most of all in a civilization founded upon

slavery. But what are we to say when Paul gives this social teaching its widest application, and abolishes in one sublime phrase all the distinctions that lay behind the national antagonisms of that ancient world? " There is neither Jew nor Greek, . . . Barbarian, Scythian, bond nor free." What idols with feet of clay this new Hammer in the hands of this new Iconoclast was to shatter to pieces ! What painstaking genius has been consecrated in subsequent centuries to the task of patching up these idols again ! " Neither Jew nor Greek." Was all that cultivation of the spirit of exclusiveness, which is commonly called patriotism, to go for nothing ? Was the Roman to have no pride of preëminence over the Barbarian ? Was the fair child of classic Greece to be regarded as on an exact equality with the swarthy and uncivilized Scythian ? Will these wild apostles of equality lay their disrespectful hands on the altars of hereditary aristocracy, social and racial, and suggest that the Roman is not to count for more than the "Angles" who are bought and sold in his slave-market ? I am speaking now of the great days when the faith was free and uncorrupt, the days before its un-holy compromises with the world, the days before, in one splendid and fatal hour, it conquered the Roman Empire and was conquered by it. I am speaking of the time of its romance, when it surrendered nothing, and never dreamed of becoming safe and tame and respectable and even fashionable; the time when it feared no one and flattered no one ; the time when its confessors were the men and women whom the world could not bully and could not buy. Then it was demonstrated that the Christian love, which is the creation of Christ, welded those who received it into a Brotherhood where external differences melted away and became non-existent, and the only realities in the world were the faith, the hope, and the love which were the enduring property of every believer.

If I seem to labour this point, it is because I touch here upon the real secret of the power which the first Christian preachers and confessors exercised, and which won their victory against such formidable odds.   They were sincerely indifferent to all that made up the ambitions of the world amid which they lived ; and this indifference to the mere externals of life gave the powers and principalities no weapon with which to assail them. Nothing in all the marvellous records stands out clearer than the sense of hopelessness and failure that gradually overwhelmed their enemies. Nothing could be done against such men as these first Christian ancestors of ours which they either feared or felt. The dignities and emoluments on which princes and governments rely, not in vain, for dealing with awkward critics, or persons of inconvenient knowledge, had no attraction for these idealists. They were supremely disinterested. You and I are so accustomed to hearing the sneer of the cynics who assume that we are no more indifferent than the rest of mankind to the luxuries and resources of civilization that we have gradually consented to their theory ; and in doing so have unintentionally impoverished our office of its kingliest power.

No cynic ever whispered such depreciation

of the men and women who held all their possessions cheap, and passed even from the mansion to the mine with serene tranquillity, turning every loss and deprivation into a sacrament. Open your Church History in its early chapters and read at random the thrilling letter of Cyprian to those ministers and members who had been condemned to labour in the mines. Some of them had been delicately nurtured. They had as much, one would suppose, to line their brows with care as the modern pastor who writes pathetically of the difficulty of " making good " in congested city or deserted village. But they certainly never pitied themselves, nor did their brethren offer them sympathy, but congratulation. Here is how Cyprian writes to them. " In the mines the body is refreshed, not by beds and pillows, but by the comforts and joys of Christ. Your limbs, wearied with labour, recline upon the earth, but it is no punishment to lie there with Christ. Your bread is scanty, but man lives not by bread alone but by the word of God. You are in want of clothing to defend you from the cold, but he who has put on Christ has clothing and ornament enough.   Even though, my dearest brethren, you cannot celebrate the communion of the Lord's Supper, your faith need feel no want.   You do celebrate the most glorious communion ; you do bring God the most costly oblation, since the Holy Scriptures declare that God will not despise a broken and a contrite spirit.   Your example has been followed by a large portion of the Church who have confessed with you and been crowned. United to you by ties of the strongest love, they could not be separated from their pastors by dungeons and mines.   Even young maidens and boys are with you.   What power have you now in a victorious conscience—what triumph in your hearts, when you can walk through the mines with enslaved bodies but with souls conscious of mastery ; when you know that Christ is with you, rejoicing in the patience of His servants, who in His footsteps and by His ways are entering into the Kingdom of eternity."

That is how Cyprian offers these disciples

and witnesses who had lost everything the world values, not his compassion but his congratulation. I am pressing upon you that the preachers of the first Christian centuries felt themselves the representatives of a new society, or as Dr. Harnack says, a new people, with unique standards. It is of immense importance that you should realize that Jews, Romans, Greeks, Barbarians, were offered citizenship in this new nation on equal terms ; and that no differences of rank, education or wealth were allowed any consideration whatsoever. Not immediately perhaps, but gradually, they came to the consciousness that they were a new world-state, destined eventually to conquer and subdue all political nations, and supply the basis of a universal civilization. You will never understand the thoughts and passions that burned and blazed in these men's souls if you do not realize something of what this conception meant to them, and how attractive it was to those who listened. Dr. Hatch of Oxford in writing upon the early Christian centuries defined the eternal mission of the Church as this—"to substitute for the socialism that is based upon the assumption of clashing interests, the socialism that is based on the sense of spiritual union."

The preachers of the apostolic age and the great centuries that followed were the heralds of that higher socialism. What their Gospel meant you can all estimate when you reflect that the members of the Roman nobility or the proudest family among the Jewish Pharisees had to confess the slave who had become a Christian as a social equal. But when you realize that, you will realize also why the ideals of the Christian society swept over the Roman Empire like a conflagration. For it is not the case in this much-maligned world, that a great human response awaits the carefully-calculated and shrewdly-balanced compromises, that aim at softening the susceptibilities of the rich without violently antagonizing the poor. The truths that conquer the world are not compromises at all, but certain splendid simplicities, not only courageously and unambiguously stated but, equally without qualification, accepted and applied. Within the borders of this new people the social contrast was unchallenged ; and the preacher could without the shadow of hypocrisy or insincerity proclaim its reality to all the world. Do you ever wonder why it is that to-day, in our championship of our faith and order, our witness sometimes falters ; that we fall back upon apologies where we need to use unconditional affirmations ? Can any preacher of to-day say from his pulpit, with the same fervour and sincerity as the first Christian preachers, that the Christian Church is a unique society of people where social distinctions do not exist, and where men and women of every race and condition may meet on the basis of absolute equality ?

Yet for that we were created. Not to accept the old standards and have imposed upon us the old distinctions of an ancient pagan civilization, but to present a society which is a new creation in Christ Jesus, and which will kindle the enthusiasm and revive the hope of those who have found neither hope nor help in any other society in the world. Much of this that I am saying may apply

less to you than to my own land.   These old
caste feelings are only slowly dissolving before the nobler democratic influences that are
now coming into play ; and many generations, and even centuries will pass before the
Christian ideal will be realized.   Any preacher
who talked of the Church as the home where
social distinctions were unknown would not
only be laughed to scorn, he would laugh
his own statement to scorn.   And the fact of
the matter is we do not realize how large a
section of Christian apologetic we have sac-
rificed ; nor how invaluable and irreplaceable
is the strategical position we have evacuated.

It is perhaps enough that I should say as
I close that this that has been called Christian Socialism springs, as every worthy socialism does, out of a high individualism—a
sense of the incalculable and imperishable
worth of the human soul.   This may seem
to some of you the most old-fashioned truth
to have thrust upon you in these modern
days, but I am certain that no preacher is going to count for much who has not seen every

soul in the world in the light of the Christ
who died for it. It seems sometimes as
if modern civilization holds some souls very
cheap. That may be. But it is the business
of the Christian preacher to stand by his
Gospel. What is that Gospel? It is con-
tained in a verse of one of the greatest Christian hymns :

> " Were the whole realm of Nature mine,
>   That were a present far too *small !*
>   Love so amazing, so Divine,
>   Demands *my Soul*—— "

That is to say that my soul is a greater
and bigger thing than "the whole realm of
nature." Do you believe it? I agree it is
the most romantic of all beliefs. It affirms
that the soul of every forced labourer on the
Amazon is of more value than all the mines
of Johannesburg, all the diamonds of Kim-
berly, all the millions of all the magnates of
America. It affirms that in God's sight all
the suns and stars that people infinite space,
are of inferior worth to one human spirit
dwelling, it may be, in the degraded body of
some victim of drink or lust, some member

of the gutter population of a great city who
has descended to his doom by means of the
multiplied temptations with which our so-
called society environs him.   It is a romantic
creed.   But if it is not true Christianity itself
is false ; and certain it is that there has never
been any triumphant Christian movement in
the history of the Church save as that high
doctrine of the human soul has been preached.
For Christianity lives by the majesty of its
beliefs.   It lives by its uncompromising truths.
It lives by demanding of its disciples, not the
minimum, but the maximum of faith and
service.

To-day we are witnessing many audacious
and inspiring endeavours to construct in this
world new and more Christian civilizations.
This principle that we hear so often on both
sides of the Atlantic, that every man, woman
and child shall have a fair chance—what
does it mean ?   Who will be the prophets
of that ideal if not ourselves ?   What argument can sustain so high and sacred a conception of duty except the argument as to
the supreme worth of each individual soul ?

It is from that that the real rights of man must spring. And for the overthrow of every system of government, or organization of society that is injurious to, or oppressive of, the individual life, this is the revolutionary doctrine that can be relied on. I charge you, as the inheritors of the peerless traditions and golden ideals of the primitive Christian society, as the modern prophets of the " new People," as the interpreters to this marvellous century of the eternal principles for which the Christian churches stand, that you steep yourselves in the thoughts and beliefs of the apostolic age, face bravely and unflinchingly their doctrines, and the social consequences of their doctrines, and that at all costs you hold back nothing of the truth for any fear or favour of man. For only thus shall we see in our time a growing reverence and enthusiasm for the Church of Christ, and the fulfillment of that hope which Dr. Hatch confessed in the most eloquent of his Bampton lectures, "a Church that shall outshine even the golden glory of its dawn by the splendour of its eternal noon."

LECTURE IV

THE ROYALTY OF THE PULPIT : ATHANASIUS AND CHRYSOSTOM

LECTURE IV

THE ROYALTY OF THE PULPIT:
ATHANASIUS AND CHRYSOSTOM

THE Christian Church has been the nursing-home of great orators. This is not wonderful. For oratory to become great, it needs the inspiration of a great cause, of great ideals. This the Christian Church supplied, with its doctrines of the All-Father, of man triumphant by faith over sin and death, and of humanity destined to become one universal family in Christ. It made an overpowering appeal to the imagination in the mystery of the Word made flesh, in Paul's doctrine of solidarity, and in the revelation of eternal life. We know that as a matter of fact, so mighty was the new inspiration beneath which the souls of men were revived, that Art, Literature, Architecture, Music were born again. When we speak of Christian Art or Christian

Literature we do so because we are sensible of a new quality in them distinguishing them from art or literature under pagan forms.

The same is true of architecture and music. The Christian cathedral is different in kind from the noblest form of classical temple. We are conscious that the soul of the architect is seeking to express higher ideals of reverence and mystical experience. The student of poetry proposes to himself as a problem what it is in Dante that touches us so much more nearly and powerfully than Vergil, why all the poetry of the ancients is pale before the disciplined emotion and passion of Milton. Music can hardly be said to have found itself, and given permanent expression to human aspiration until it became the handmaid of Christianity, and gave utterance to the depths of human grief and heights of human rapture in the Oratorio and the Mass. To-day I ask you to believe, that this new inspiration of which Christ Jesus was the author, created also a new order of speakers, a new type of oratory. If I speak of Christian eloquence, it is because I believe that the highest type of eloquence the world has ever known is inseparable from the most exalted inspiration and can only flow from that source.

This is not said to depreciate the glorious philippics of Demosthenes, or the orations of Cicero, the two outstanding orators of the classic ages. But splendid as Cicero's speeches are, and worthy of your study as masterpieces of forensic eloquence with their invective, their argument, their satire, their wit, their occasional high ethical appeal, they do not stir the deepest emotions of our souls, or inspire in us the loftiest vision. The orations of Demosthenes are the utterances not only of a supreme rhetorician, but of a true prophet and a great patriot. In his passionate devotion to the liberties of his people he is one of the immortals. The glow of his heroic spirit is in his words still, and will keep them alive forever. But all local patriotism however deep and fervent must be inferior in real greatness to that patriotism to the kingdom of God which is the creation, I say it reverently, of the genius of our Lord, and possessed by which men transcend their local racial distinctions, and realize their brotherhood with all humanity. When a soul speaks to us great enough to be illuminated by that ideal, and noble enough to be fired by that enthusiasm, he becomes the standing demonstration of the superiority of the power of Christianity, the universal religion, over every localized or nationalized form of religion whatsoever.

I ask your attention at this lecture to two great masters of rhetoric, admirable illustrations of the romance of preaching, whose astonishing careers provide innumerable lessons for the modern preacher. The two I refer to are Athanasius and Chrysostom. I associate them not so much because they were almost contemporaries in that critical fourth century, but because they were so dissimilar in the externals of their ministry while exemplifying so vividly the same supreme power of inspired personality. We shall see that so far as outward advantages

are concerned, Chrysostom had everything
that Athanasius lacked. Nature had fash-
ioned him to be an orator. He was tall and
commanding in figure, handsome in features,
with a magnificent organ-voice, and a flow
of words which no other orator could rival.
So far as education was concerned he had
passed through the discipline of a legal
training, and had won distinction at the bar
before he was carried by irresistible sympathies into the service of the Church. We
see the result of his legal practice in that
lucid and cogent forensic style which made
his expositions of Scripture so fascinating,
and left the hearers without an answer.

But there is a vast difference between
Chrysostom the legal pleader and Chrysostom the Christian pleader. Chrysostom's
homilies are an exalted form of argumenta-
tive discourse ; and it is the sacred passion
that throbs through his periods that, even
more than his rhetorical felicities, captures
our interest still. Over against the royal
figure of the golden-mouthed prince of
preachers stands the one whose name and

fame overtopped that of emperors and military conquerors, but whose unparallelled ascendancy over his fellows was due wholly to spiritual, and in no degree to physical, properties. Ernest Renan described St. Paul, in one of those fierce phrases that live, as an " ugly little Jew." Athanasius was apparently a dwarf, shortening by a stoop even the squat figure. His nose was hooked, and he wore a stubby, bristling beard. His hair was apparently straw-coloured. It is surely not in such a guise that Mr. Bernard Shaw would have us recognize the super-man ; and I suspect that many college committees might have hesitated long before accepting for the ministry one who would have required some mechanical means to add a cubit to his stature, before he could even have been seen over the side of any ordinary pulpit.

Yet super-man he was. I like to read how that strange countenance was illuminated to seraphic beauty by light of inward holiness and zeal for truth. Such was the mighty soul in the attenuated body of him who dared emperors and defied ecclesiastics, who was exiled again and again and again and yet again, who was as much at home in the caves of the Egyptian deserts as in the council-chamber of Nicæa or the palace of Alexandria.   No man was less depressed by defeat, or exalted by success.   Yet the gorgeous annals of Constantine afford no parallel to the splendour of popular triumph, when Alexandria swept out beyond its walls to welcome back its banished preacher and bishop, the multitude of its people suggesting to an eye-witness the Nile overflowing its banks. Then came stepping along the sandy road out of the wilderness of his exile, the strange dwarf figure, with the beard whitened with toil and care, but the face still radiant, and the light in the eyes that told of the unconquerable soul.   No modern preacher, with any pride in his sublime calling, can ever omit to do reverence at that niche in the great temple of prophets where the statue stands of

" Royal-hearted Athanase
By Paul's own mantle blest."

If only we could extract from the pages of history or extort by some scientific process the secret of that magical fact we call *person-ality!* But in default of that, we may surely be pardoned for doubting whether any man is going to make more of the ministry than a very commonplace and even humdrum affair who has never been set on fire. It may be doubted whether all the modern athletic experts can add a cubit to our stature, and in any case, the conquest of the world does not depend upon it. Less and less will mere physical qualities, or mere brute force, stand for empire in the affairs of men; and this I venture to say who am nevertheless keenly alive to all the joys of bodily existence, and advantages of a trained physique. But *the one supreme qualification for the ministry is a soul of flame.* Helen Keller may be blind and deaf and dumb, but she has preached faith and courage and love all round the world; while millions of men and women of no physical defect whatsoever have never had any message to which it was worth while for any one to listen. The power to kindle the spirits of our fellows is the endowment for which we pray and plead. I am well aware that no class-room can give it. Even amid the intellectual interests of university life, and the vivid enthusiasms of youth, it may be lost and not found. The minister who has it, carries with him everywhere the argument from which there is no appeal. The minister who has it not may labour pathetically with the tools of logic and rhetoric but at the end he will be desolate of spirit because of the little that his hands have built.

It is an old story this, yet we cannot get away from it, that the world bows before *soul*. What it wants to know about our religion is not so much that it is *reasonable* as that it is *real*. One of Athanasius' enemies wrote about him that he was "a dwarf and no man"; but once Athanasius rose to defend the faith that was dearer than his life and he was a man of giant stature and no dwarf. Vast audiences that were tempted to laugh at his puny figure and mean appearance, drew faith and hope and love and zeal from the Christ-illuminated soul of this apostolic preacher.

I would commend the study of Athanasius
to any one who has not formed the true idea
in his mind of the *royalty of the pulpit*, and
that it is to be maintained in this world as the
one place where the truth of God is to be
proclaimed without fear or favour. Woe to
that preacher who does not keep within his
breast an incorruptible conscience, whose
vision of God is clouded by unworthy fear of
his audience, and whose self-respect is under-
mined by unmanly compromises and sur-
renders to placate wealthy or influential
patrons! Everybody knows the temptation
to substitute for the high and difficult vocation of a prophet of Truth, the amiable ambition to please a congregation. Many well-
meaning ministers have spent weary years
cajoling and flattering their people, softening
down the rebukes of the Gospel, and lining
Christ's hard sayings with velvet till the most
touchy consciences in the pews of Christendom can come in contact with them without
a shock. It might seem as if some preachers
had laid down as a law for themselves to
make nobody uncomfortable whose income

was more than £200 ($1000) a year. Quite
recently I heard a sermon on luxury in a fashionable West-End church in London ; and as
the preacher took pains to explain that Christ's
life was so different from ours that we could
not imitate its externals, I was conscious of
that pleasant rustle of silk and satin which
gently indicated the relief of the hearers. I
doubt whether anything has done so much
harm to the pulpit as the impression which
has gone abroad, that we preachers do not
face the tremendous sayings of Christ with
real faith and courage, but rather that we fall
back on critical theories, and explain to our
amenable congregations that the more difficult commands of Christ are probably textual
corruptions due to a later and ascetic age,
and in any case need not vex the peace or
alter the conduct of the twentieth century.
Yet these sayings of Jesus blaze and burn.
What use is our New Testament if it is not a
very furnace of Truth into which men's souls
are plunged and purified, and saved so as by
fire ?

I have no belief whatever in ascetic and

monastic systems, which seem to me to require an unchristian, and even anti-Christian theory of life. But I confess to you I am impressed by the fact that both Athanasius and Chrysostom had a monastic preparation for their public ministry. Youth needs to be austere with itself. Self-discipline can be learned in better places than the cell of the anchorite, but it must be learned if the ministry is not to make shipwreck. These men learned how to do without things; they learned to be content with simplicity; they learned that life "consisteth not in the abundance of the things a man possesseth." They definitely crucified some of the subordinate ambitions. They got fairly through the crust of civilization and made contact with the realities that lie at its heart. Such men when they come to deal with shams and illusions are apt to be severe iconoclasts, like Elijah and John the Baptist, but they know how to sear men's souls and shake their consciences.

Sometimes I am tempted to think that the defect of our modern ministerial preparation for the ministry is that we have too much to enjoy and too little to endure. When we go out into the arena our thews and sinews are too soft; and in the first shock we go down in the dust, and sometimes it takes bitter years to find our feet. When we are dependent on the superfluities of life we are not so likely to be able to speak out our truth, if by so doing we may be in danger of losing them.

Do not let me be misunderstood. I am the last man to underrate to you the virtues of tact and discretion. It was Athanasius' distinction that his own people loved him and trusted him without reserve. He had the two endowments with which any minister can go far—common sense and the gift of humour. Besides, I think too highly of mankind to believe that as a rule they resent the ministry that deals faithfully and affectionately with them. Dr. Dale used to say that people talked of saying *faithful* things when they meant saying *disagreeable* things; and the communicated love of Christ to our hearts ought ever to forbid us to be censorious, offensive and truculent where our duty is to speak the truth with love. I have not intended to leave that side of things out of sight. But if Athanasius and his heroic ministry has one message more than another for us, it is as to the sovereignty of the Truth we hold over all human souls, and the royalty of the preacher's office when he knows that God has given to him a message which all without distinction must hear and heed.

The second aspect of Athanasius' ministry which I would ask you to consider is *the preacher as controversialist*. When we take down our histories and read the extraordinary story of how an abstract theological proposition, framed in the curiously flabby mind of Arius, set the world on fire, we are oppressed by a sense of despair of ever being able to understand an age in which such things could be. Neither do the facts become more intelligible as we see how secular policies were affected by it, and the fortunes of an empire fluctuated as the Arian tide flowed or ebbed. But after all, human destinies are settled in the world of thought and ideas. The doctrine of Homoousianism in the mouth of Athanasius

meant the unity of empire even as the word
Justification on the lips of Luther meant the
Reformation of Europe and a free Western
civilization. Faber threw into the verse of a
hymn a great truth when he wrote :

> " Workman of God ! oh lose not heart,
> *But learn what God is like ;*
> And in the darkest battle-field
> Thou shalt know where to strike."

That is why I take it the first content of
the Church's consciousness must be to know
" what God is like " ; otherwise its very fighting power is paralyzed, and its blows are
aimed uncertainly. It does not surprise me,
therefore, that the first great controversy in
the Christian Church should be in regard to
the nature of God ; and we shall generally be
agreed that as against the crude and fatuous
theory of Arius, Athanasius' protest for the
unity of the Godhead was infinitely more noble and dignified ; even as the orations of
Athanasius are a monument of massive
thought and argument in comparison with
the dervish-like jingles in which Arius en-
deavoured to popularize his pet heresy. But

it is quite true that from the far shore on
which we stand we look across "the dark
backward and abysm of time," and see those
ages of theological cyclone and volcanic action with wondering gaze. That is very
largely because we have ourselves fallen upon
the inglorious days of Quietism. It is a
strange irony if you come to think of it that
sluggishness and apathy mark our religious
life to-day in what we speak of as the strenuous West, and that this great Arian controversy was fought out with frenzied fervour in
what we speak of as the still and tranquil
Orient. Certainly the Orient was not sluggish
and stagnant when Athanasius was fighting
the world for his faith.

You remember the cynic historian's description of how the great problems laid
their grip of every huckster in the market-
place, who, before he served you with mer-
chandise, or counted out your small change,
would demand your opinion as to the relations of the Persons of the Godhead. Very
likely, I grant, to produce a plague of theological prigs! But would it do us any harm

to-day, in your land or in mine, if some great
question of eternal things were once again to
be supreme, and to awaken in the chattering
chaffering crowds of the market-places a
higher curiosity? Is it after all so noble
and superior an attitude of mind, this modern
one of ours, that nothing matters ; that high
thoughts about Deity are wasted time ; that
sublime speculations and doctrinal controversies are the signs of an inferior and de-
generate age? I am not here to apologize
for the controversial language of Athanasius.
Dean Stanley made a careful but not ex-
haustive collection of his favourite epithets
for his theological opponents—" devils, anti-
christs, maniacs, Jews, polytheists, atheists,
dogs, wolves, lions, hares, chameleons, hy-
dras, eels, cuttlefish, gnats, beetles, leeches."
His vocabulary, it is plain, might have won
for him distinction in a political career.

But in theology to-day we have reached
serene heights of unruffled calm. The chaste
soul of the most definite of our modern dog-
matists would never be conscious of sufficient
provocation to depart from the language of

self-possession and politeness even if he indubitably believed that the errors of some
other teacher were poisoning men's souls.
But do we not suggest a contrast? Theology to-day is for the most part a product
of the academic life. In the days of Athanasius it was hammered out in the wilderness
and the cell. Men forged their beliefs, like
thunderbolts, at the centre of the storm. The
faiths that clothed their souls were tested in
the furnace heated sevenfold. You can still
tell the difference between the article of a
creed cunningly worded to evade a difficulty, conciliate a doubter or confound an
enemy, and an affirmation which is the cry
of a great soul for some truth which is a
fixed star in its firmament and without which
it will blunder along its way. It is this passionate sincerity that lends dignity to controversy. As we read the story, all Athanasius' extravagances and personalities drop
away from him, and we only see the prophet
who cared so supremely for the glory of his
God and the honour of his Saviour, that he
was prepared to stand alone against the

world, until the truth he saw was recognized and acknowledged by all.

My brethren, it is an open question with me whether either the evils of controversy or the gains of compromise are as great as we often think them.   Controversy is noble or ignoble according to the spirit in which it is conducted.   What is referred to, *ad nauseam*, as the virtue of compromise and accommodation usually means the painful discovery of some colourless and almost meaningless formula in which two antagonistic ideas, whittled down to their minimum, are supposed to be peaceably interred.   I am always comforted to know that you cannot really bury any belief *alive*.   You cannot bury it until you can truly say, " peace to *its ashes*."   It belongs to the glory of Athanasius that, even living when he did, he had no belief in the coercion of conscience by force. He was, rather, like the dear old priest in Praed's poem, who

> " Held, in spite of all his learning,
>   That if a man's belief is bad
>   It will not be improved by burning."

This zealot for truth, and even for dogma, believed in fighting his battle out with the weapon of argument, reason and persuasion, and winning the only victory that is honourable to a Christian combatant. Nobody expects that our battles of to-day or to-morrow will prove a reproduction of the old Arian strife; though there are more unlikely things than a keen revival one of these days of a controversy as to the being of God and the nature of the relations between the Father and the Son. But if it should not be your lot to live through an age of theological dispute, there are other controversies upon us in which the knights of the Church of Jesus may not refuse to quit them like men. There has never been a generation yet in which the Lord has not had a controversy with His people; and it is a test of our right to be where we are, whether we hear the Lord's controversy or not. We cannot rank ourselves under the Christian flag without conceding certain human rights, which no existing social system that I know of, adequately and practically interprets.

The contrast between the Sermon on the Mount and a civilization like that of Europe, based on force and fear, does not grow less violent as our people become more intelligent. Nor can a civilization that includes the extremes of pampered luxury and grinding poverty live in the light of a renascent Christian ethics. Controversy there must be on behalf of the unity of humanity as strong and uncompromising as Athanasius ever waged for the unity of Deity. When many of you go forth to the field where in Milton's words "immortal garlands are to be won *not without dust and heat*"; when in the war for Christian Righteousness as well as for the Christian Faith you flash your maiden swords, I can only beseech you that the spirit of your warfare may be the spirit which our Captain made unique—a love that no bitterness can alienate, a peace that no strife can disturb, and a gaiety of soul which can take the rubs and knocks without melancholy, acrimony, or self-pity.

I turn now to a brief consideration of the life and work of Chrysostom, who has al-

ways enjoyed a place of preëminence among
Christian preachers and the world's famous
orators, and who may suggest many lessons
to the more ambitious among us who are
resolved to achieve and to practice the craft
of a master of assemblies. So far as I know,
Chrysostom was the first preacher to bring to
the service of the Gospel all the arts of
oratory which are relied upon in the law-
courts and the forum. Nobody knew better
than he how to take captive the intellects of
his hearers in the toils of a closely-knit argument ; and, indeed, it would be true to say
that he observed the golden rule that rhetoric
should always be the servant of logic, even
as in a great picture the absence of accuracy
of drawing and perspective can never be
wholly atoned for by the most resplendent
colouring. First of all, he knew clearly
where he was going, and saw to it that his
hearers could not fail to know. Afterwards
he devoted all the resources of his knowledge and imagination to add to the interest
and profit of the journey. He must indeed
have been a formidable critic and antagonist,

for his powers of irony and satire were un-
rivalled, and no person in high place who
came under his scathing censures was ever
likely to forget it. Satire is a dangerous
weapon to handle ; and only a kindly and
genial form of it is ever likely to produce a
Christian end in repentance or conversion ;
and perhaps in his last years of exile and
persecution, Chrysostom himself may have
wondered whether other weapons than the
lash of fiery and sarcastic speech might not
have profited the kingdom of God more.
Moreover, if satire is always a questionable
instrument for achieving the real ends of
preaching, rhetoric is equally an indulgence
that needs to be carefully guarded. Chrysostom's courage in rebuking the Empress
Eudocia was admirable, but his task would
have been many times easier if he had not
allowed himself to be carried away at first on
the tide of rhetoric, to inflated and fulsome
panegyric and adulation.

Having uttered those two warnings, I go
on to say that Chrysostom's style is a model
of what Christian eloquence at its highest

can be. You and I live in a time when, as I
shall often have occasion to insist, the preacher
has lost the sense of the splendour and
romance of his calling. This loss has affected
us in many ways. The colours have faded
out of our sky. The universe has turned
gray around us. The glory and radiance of
the dawn have suffered some eclipse. Our
range of vision, and our confidence of victory
are alike attenuated. In consequence, that
highest form of rhetoric which is the glow
and poetry of faith and enthusiasm becomes
almost impossible to us. For rhetoric is the
natural language of emotion and imagination. Where there is no real depth of feeling
it is artificial and stilted and tiresome. But
when the passion of the heart is strong and
deep it will express itself with some splendour
of Pre-Raphaelite colouring. The preacher
has never really been thrilled by the ideal of
his vocation who has not wanted to set it to
music, as Robert Burns set Nature to song,
or as Turner transferred her glories to canvas.

It is hardly necessary to say that the rhetoric of Chrysostom has little or nothing in

common with that disease of the pulpit egoist which manifests itself in pretentiousness and polysyllables. If you want the model of peerless eloquence it is to be found in the most familiar passage of the New Testament, and it may interest you to count the words which are of more than one syllable, " Come unto Me, all ye that labour and are heavy laden, and I will give you rest. Take My yoke upon you and learn of Me, for I am meek and lowly of heart, and ye shall find rest unto your souls. For My yoke is easy and My burden is light." There are great passages in Lincoln and in Bright—our two supreme modern masters of Saxon speech— which are as simple as this, and yet similarly charged with emotion that leaves none of us unaffected. No, rhetoric is a nobler thing than the turgid recital of redundant epithets and high-sounding substantives. To how small a modicum of thought can some rhetorical efforts be reduced when you have shaken the sawdust out! But as against the modern taste for Christianity in capsules, and for the tersest, most prosaic and least emotional statement of fact and argument, I do venture to break a lance for Chrysostom.

The supreme merit of Chrysostom is that he never for one moment forgets that he is dealing with human beings and human life. He is not solely concerned with making good certain logical or theological propositions. While his legal training is invaluable to him, his is no narrow canonistical intellect, nor is his outlook upon mankind less human because of the careful development of his reasoning powers. Before his eyes the great pageantry of the people's life always moves ; and in his sermons you will find a vivid picture of his times. On his canvas are brilliant splashes of colour ; for it was his object to hold up the mirror to the multitude and compel them to see what their existence was like. It has been truly said that the pages of Chrysostom present us with a "cosmical panorama." The pomp and pride of the Imperial court, and the luxurious mode of life of an Oriental aristocracy are so powerfully portrayed, that after fifteen hundred years you can almost hear the strains of music at some princely banquet or be conscious of the perfumes that scented the raiment of the feasters. Equally lifelike are his descriptions of the hippodrome, with its wild scenes of racing and gaming; while, if I may quote again, "Even the rope-dancers, jugglers, conjurers, fortune-tellers, buffoons, mountebanks mingled with grave philosophers with long beards, staff and cloak, were grouped together in his homiletical sketches."

Here lies his charm and his power. This man of giant brain, and legal and monastic training, is nevertheless himself a human being, with a warm heart and wide knowledge of his brothers and sisters in the life of his city. He has mingled with them in their pleasures, has pitied their follies, sympathized with their temptations, trembled for their sins, wept with them for their griefs, and laughed with them in their frolics and diversions. The people flocked to him and hung upon his lips, not only because of his oratory, but because he knew them so well, loved them so much, and talked to them about those actual homely facts of daily life which make up the greater part of every one's existence.

Here then we have two qualities in Chrysostom which in their combination make him unique—he is a *Man of the Word and a Man of the World*. The Homilies of Chrysostom are to me a phenomenal production. In their close and minute analysis of Scripture, and courage of exposition they are an anticipation of the best modern criticism. Chrysostom himself is saturated with the Scripture, and is determined that his audiences shall be taught to base their lives upon the principle of Holy Writ. In those days when the writings of the New Testament were comparatively so recent, and were so little known to the masses, this great preacher felt that their best hope of progress lay in their systematic education in the letter and spirit of the Scriptures of our faith. He thus made himself the popular interpreter of the Christian documents, always endeavouring to get at the exact sense, and to preach the truth honestly and fearlessly. At the same time by virtue of his catholic experience he

is, in the best sense of a much-abused term,
a man of the world; and he is resolute to
apply the Gospel ethics over the whole wide
area of human life and affairs. That is why
he must know at first hand, life at the court,
life in the bazaars, life at the games, and life
in the streets, the school, the homes of the
people. Again and again we find him, with
all his admiration for the devout monk, pro-
testing that Christ's laws and privileges are
for all men and women without exception
and " not for solitaries only." If it be not
possible, he argues, in the secular life, and in
wedded life, to attain the Beatitudes, then
Christ has destroyed, and not saved, all men.
No preacher in all the Christian ages had a
clearer conception of the great truth that the
Evangel of Life in Christ is for all people,
at all times and in all places, and that no
exigencies of business, politics or pleasure
can relieve any of us of the duty of obedience
to the laws of the kingdom of God.

I notice further for our own instruction that
the Homilies of Chrysostom are not the expositions of a *lecturer*, but, what is very differ-

ent, the expositions of a *preacher*. There is
a very wide contrast between one who is only
a teacher, an expositor, a lecturer, an essayist,
and one who is a preacher and a prophet.
It has always seemed to me that there is
much force in the modern appeal for more
expository preaching. I only submit that it
must be *preaching*. The class-room is one
place, the pulpit is another. The closest
possible application is needful in the study
if we are to be sound interpreters of the
Gospel; and the new Renaissance which
some of us will live to see, when the interest
of the people will be rekindled in the best
and greatest of all books, may very likely
come along the line of systematic and scientific exposition. But we have got to *preach*
our exposition. I mean, that the same passion for souls, the same constraining love of
humanity, must burn and glow in our expository discourses that make it possible to
warm our hearts at Chrysostom's Homilies
to the present day. Men must be brought
to see that in the Bible one end is sought by
divers means and in divers portions, and that

end is the salvation and happiness of all
mankind.   In other words if the world is
to be interested in the Bible, it must be convinced that the Bible is interested in the
world ; and that the modern world is made
up of just the same great root problems of
life and death, joy and sorrow, vice and
virtue that Isaiah wrestled with, and on
which the Lord Christ shed His ineffable
and unfading light.

The advent of Chrysostom is, I think, the
dawn of a new epoch in preaching.   True,
there is nothing new in the authority which
he asserted for his message.   In his courage
and freedom in dealing with the wealthy and
highly-placed he was the worthy contempo-
rary of Athanasius.   There was nothing new
in the risks he ran, or the afflictions he suffered.   He was one of those who well knew
that the preacher's lot is a desperate war
with organized evil and throned iniquity.
The length of his public ministry is a tribute
to his moral ascendancy.   But we are not as-
tonished, though we may stand aghast, when
at last the forces of hell are let loose upon

him, and once more in history Jezebel drives
Elijah to exile and the desert, though in this
case the prophet was to return no more.
The long-drawn-out agony of his last exile it
is not for me to describe. He died in that
same far lone spot among the mountains of
Asia Minor, where many centuries afterwards
another martyr-evangelist, Henry Martyn,
burned out for God. His dust rested there
until the day when with pontifical splendour
amid the tears and reverence of a subsequent
generation and solemn prayers and penances
of princes and people, it was translated to
the City of Constantine where the better part
of his life-work had been done.

It has been my aim that the significant
facts about these two great pulpit orators
should emphasize themselves for us without
my italicizing them. But perhaps by way of
summary I may gather together two or three
suggestions that are well worth your consideration. I think we want a new pulpit oratory that will be free from the vice of turgid
rhetoric, but that will be the rich fruit of a new

vision of our world-conquering Faith. Something has got to happen to us; some magic change must pass over our spirits; and beneath the inspiration of the new revelation of Deity and Humanity our speech will clothe itself with colour and beauty as naturally and inevitably as the spring adorns and decorates the earth. I am one of those who believe that the churches have never been so rich in scholarship, and so competent in criticism. But I am not sure that any human being has been inspired to attempt the heights of love and life because he has been thrilled with the realization of the composite character of the Book of Genesis. Science is the one authority left, I know, to which we all do obeisance, and in the presence of which we take off our shoes from our feet. But I sometimes imagine the mere scientist standing in the presence of the wonder and glory of Niagara, with its flashing, flying waters, and iridescent waves, and summing it all up in the terse and eloquent formula H_2O. I am all for scientific accuracy and precision; but I confess that the Bible is more to me than is summed

up in the formulas of critical analysis. Its
magic, its mystery, its poetry, its glory escape the skill of those patient investigators
who track its secret in the dissecting room.
Athanasius' theology may have been wrong ;
but nothing can destroy the fact that he trod
the desert as he trod the marble halls of
princes bathed in the light that never was on
sea or land. Let us be quite certain that in
our honest ambition to understand all mysteries and all knowledge we are not strangers
to that experience of the Love Divine of
which there is no scientific explanation possible except that it is shed abroad in our
hearts by the Holy Spirit that is given unto
us.

Once more, let us think of these two great
apostles together. If I may make the rough
distinction, Athanasius preached more about
Deity and Chrysostom more about humanity.
Chrysostom I think knew men better, and
Athanasius I think knew God better. I have
spoken to little purpose if I have failed to
bring home to my hearers, that I believe we
need men in the ministry who know and

sympathize with human life in all its phases. But to-day I close upon the other note. It is much easier to talk about men than to talk about God. It is a rarer thing to find in the pulpit a man whose mind moves naturally and easily in the sublimest of all themes and experiences, than to find a man in the pulpit who can talk wisely and helpfully about human life. But it is the condemnation of the Christian preacher when his audience comes to feel that though he knows them very well, he cannot teach them to know God, whom to know is life eternal. Wordsworth's lark, as you remember, with nest upon the earth, was nevertheless born to the freedom of the upper air, and knew the secret of the infinite blue, and the Christian prophet and orator of to-morrow, I doubt not, must equally be master of the two worlds

" True to the kindred points of Heaven and Home."

LECTURE V

THE RULERS OF PEOPLES: SAVONAROLA, CALVIN AND JOHN KNOX

LECTURE V

THE RULERS OF PEOPLES: SAVO-
NAROLA, CALVIN AND JOHN KNOX

IT should never be forgotten that the
preacher's message has a *timeless* and
a *timely* element in it. Clearly, the historical facts on which our faith is built cannot be one thing in one generation and another in another; though our interpretations
of the facts may and will change, and our applications of the teachings they convey will
change also. It is written in the book of
Psalms, in what I have often felt was an inspired mistranslation, " Because they have no
changes, therefore they fear not God." The
meaning of that seemingly cryptic saying
would appear to be that we cannot really be
reverent of God's law of life and progress, the
law of growth, unless we are prepared for
new formulas and new forms under which the
Truth may find expression. Whenever a
Christian preacher and the church to which

he ministers are unprogressive, the interest taken by the outside public in their existence becomes mainly an antiquarian one. They are no longer reckoned among those living forces that mould our thought, shape our institutions, and inspire our ideals. We hear a great deal about our historic faith, and much stress is laid upon the fact that we have nearly two thousand years of eventful history behind us.

But that is an argument that clearly has no weight against the devotees of religions which are indefinitely more ancient. I hope it is not straining a point to say, that the charm of Christianity is not in its antiquity but in its novelty ; not in the fact that it is aged and reverend, but in the fact that it is eternally young. I say nothing of those strange souls, who are so profoundly uneasy in the life of to-day, and who ever turn their wistful eyes backwards to the paradise of the Middle Ages. They are not of their century, and the century does not belong to them. But the real Church of God ever walks the world with the tireless step, the eyes forward—gazing eyes, and the mobile receptive spirit of youth. If ever the disciples of Christ were to become a society in which the ennuis and dubieties of the world were to eat like acid into its enthusiasms and its faiths, it is quite clear that Christianity would be at the end of its conquests. What all other religions, societies and institutions envy us, is the magic of rejuvenation. So far from transformations and renaissances having any terror for us we know that with us they belong to the nature of things. History has in this respect a heartening tale to tell. Christendom has again and again, if I may use the apostolic language, been " transformed by the renewal of the mind."

Great and beneficent changes of doctrine have swept over Europe. New truths have arisen whose evangelists have forsaken everything, yea life itself, to make them the permanent heritage of Christ's people. And with these renewals of the faith and thought of Christendom there has gone equally radical reconstruction of her institutions. All this means that Christianity has possessed to a supreme degree that power of adaptation to changing needs and conditions which is the accepted scientific law of life and growth. When the great apostle declared, "I am become all things to all men if by any means I may save some," he laid down the principle of Christian opportunism. He was not leaving out of account the unchangeable and timeless element in his ministry, but he was taking count of the timely element. He boasted, as you remember, of his own versatility. He could become as a Greek to the Greek, as a Roman to the Roman, as a Jew to the Jew. He made it his business to understand his audiences, to meet them on their own ground, and to appreciate different points of view. Especially in dealing with his avowed antagonists, he was resolved to know their beliefs, their prejudices, their passions, so that in the science of "parry and thrust" he should not find himself "beating the air." That was why Paul did not hesitate to withstand Peter to his face, in defense of freedom, and over against the theory that it is the business of Christianity to impose uniformity of custom and ceremony upon men and women of diverse races and manners of life. It was the common sense of the apostle Paul, and the tenacity with which he clung to the principle of opportunism that saved Christendom, and made a world-wide evangelism possible. Again and again, the largest interests of the kingdom have been safeguarded by those heroic preachers who had the soul of romance in them, and who would not be bound hand and foot by ecclesiastical red-tape.

The great merit of Paul's audacious policy was, that he was a strategist who thought out his strategy on the actual field of war, and not in some remote Jerusalem war-office where parchment and sealing-wax were more plentiful than experience and foresight. The most fatal of all the Church's dreams has been the dream of uniformity. Even Paul's splendid courage and example were not equal to ridding the Church of this dangerous delusion. But this we can say : all those spiritual leaders, in whom the fires of the Gospel have manifestly burned, even when they have been

most reverent of authority, have found some
way out of the fetters and manacles that
chafed their limbs and limited their activity.
Thus Xavier and St. Francis could not be re-
strained from transgressing the strict order
of the Church of Rome; nor Wesley and
Whitefield abandon their inspired errand because its fulfillment meant the violation of
those supposed decencies and proprieties
which had made the Anglicanism of their day
so prim and safe, so dull and dead. To the
apostles of uniformity everything is regulated
by unchangeable routine. There is no room
for surprises. All departures from precedent
are extravagances. The spirit of God is carefully restricted to well-defined functions, and
within a limited area. Hence the spiritual
life of the people of God must not overflow
the appointed channels.

Such is the theory of ecclesiasticism. But
the prophet is the one man who upsets the
calculations of the prelate. He is the man of
soul with a genius for the unexpected and the
unprecedented. He is a spiritual Samson
who is never happier in mind than when he

is bound with the futile withes of the Philistines. And I make bold to say that the greatest fact in Christian history is not the authority of the priest but the authority of the prophet. I do not underrate the prodigious power of ecclesiasticism. It has often been cruelly and mercilessly exercised, and the measure of external conformity that it has enforced has been very great. But the prophet has wielded a mightier power; for he has swayed the inner world of men's consciences, intellects and souls. He has governed and guided motives. He has inspired ideals of life and service. And in that way, without the mailed arm of material force, he has set in motion beneficent reformations and even revolutions, and has more profoundly influenced and affected the world-movements which make human history what it is, than all the power of the ecclesiastical machine.

It is my intention in this lecture, to invite your consideration to three outstanding examples of Christian preachers who veritably became the conscience of the communities where they laboured, and the people for whose souls they watched as those that must give account. Each of these preachers dominated the life of a commonwealth. Each of them in his day of power reduced all other figures in the land to insignificance, and ruled the life of the people from the pulpit as from a throne. The three of whom I propose to speak are Savonarola of Florence, John Calvin of Geneva, and John Knox of Scotland.

And first, of the martyr of Florence. I have little to do with Savonarola's wonderful life-story save as it concerns the man as preacher. But it may be said that three great facts determined the form of his ministry—the shameless corruption in the Church, the open profligacy and sinful luxury of the ruling classes, and the renaissance of art and learning. Savonarola's sensitive temperament was profoundly affected by all these signs of the times. It was his cross to live and bear witness in days when the princes of the Church outvied, in greed and lust and passion, the princes of the State. He was one of many

who fled to the cloister as to a sanctuary
to escape the contagion of the plague of
immorality. He was driven across the
Apennines to Florence by the scourge of
war wielded by the merciless hand of an
arrogant and ambitious "Vicar of Christ,"
who actually died of grief and rage because
of the conclusion of peace.

From Sixtus IV to the dissolute Inno-
cent VIII and the infamous Alexander VI,
it was Savonarola's melancholy fate to live
through the period when the apostle's lurid
description of the adversaries of the true
faith was most perfectly fulfilled—"world-
rulers of this darkness, and spiritual hosts of
wickedness in heavenly places." Little
wonder that the monasteries were filled by
those who were driven there by despair, or
that Savonarola was one of them. Neither
did the new culture at first affect the pulpit
for good. It bred affectation of learning.
It had its fruit in the scholastic temper and
speech. It enriched the artificial orations of
windy rhetoricians with obscure and sometimes even obscene illustrations from the

classics. The pulpiteer with a thin veneer
of scholarship became the plague of the
Church; and when you have a whole generation of preachers who care more for
prettinesses of composition than for the cure
of souls, religion ceases to be a spiritual
force, and is regarded only with pity and
contempt. Students of the dark age through
which Savonarola prophesied, are moved to
wonder that seemingly there were no real
tears in the soul of any priest in the land,
save in Savonarola's alone.

The realization of the sin and shame of
Church and State alike affected him with
horror and anguish. But it is worth our
while to remember, that the one man who
really cared for the well-being of Florence
and of Italy, was the man there was least
eagerness to hear. Savonarola had the
bitter and humiliating experience of seeing
his congregation diminish almost to vanish-
ing point, and to hear the complaint under
which many a thoughtful earnest preacher
has suffered, that he did not cultivate the
necessary arts and graces that can alone

commend him to a congregation. He saw
the masters of a histrionic style who tickled
the ears of their hearers with their shallow
artifices, addressing crowds of hearers who
were well pleased with an entertainment that
made no demand upon intellect or conscience.
But he who sought to bring the light of Holy
Writ to bear on the burdens and miseries of
humanity, to plead for purity and freedom,
and to reason of judgment to come was
advised to practice more graces of speech.
To Savonarola it was as if a land was being
devastated by man-devouring dragons, while
the anointed St. Georges rained polished
epigrams, and clever jests at the monsters,
instead of girding on a sword of stout steel,
and making at them in the name of God. Not
that Savonarola was unaffected by the new
learning.   It helped him to see to the heart of
the Scriptures.   It loosened his obstinate at-
tachment to the traditions of the Church.   It
compelled him to face many problems of
thought which he would otherwise have
evaded. If he never reached a very con-
sistent position as a theologian, it was be-

cause his powers were mortgaged to other
purposes ; and in his desperate fight for
moral and social righteousness he had little
leisure to examine whither his intellectual
independence was leading him.

But one thing is certain. Savonarola's
ultimate triumph as a preacher is *the triumph of naturalism in the pulpit.* He
scorned the tricks and sophisms of those
who won a cheap and fleeting popularity,
but who exercised no lasting influence. He
set himself to reach and stimulate the withered, wizened conscience of the multitude ;
and to do it he relied on the instrument
of plain, searching, passionate speech. To
quote his own words which are worthy of
your attention, " These verbal elegancies and
ornaments will have to give way to sound
doctrine simply preached."   Do not misunderstand him. The idolatry of simplicity
may be carried too far. The great moving
discourses which swept all Florence subse-
quently into the cathedral to sit at Savonarola's feet, were surprisingly simple and
direct and scriptural, but the passion of the

preacher expressed itself in the irresistible rush of his flaming sentences which no soul could face and remain unscathed.

Savonarola is an easily vulnerable person to the armchair critic. His philosophy is unconvincing, his visions often took the place of argument, his ecclesiastical position was to the end ambiguous. The censor of the pulpit finds many of his most powerful and famous sermons turgid, and complains that there is too little light and shade. I am not attempting an apology for Savonarola ; but I may be allowed to point out that the test of a good sermon is not that it satisfies certain canons of style, but that it achieves certain moral and spiritual ends ; and I may also be allowed to doubt whether his latter-day critics would have done better than he in rousing Florence from her turpitude and stagnancy, and recreating the ancient civic spirit. His power lay in the realization of the magnitude of the struggle, and that only by the uttermost devotion could Christ's victory be won. He urged every believer to seek "that Christ's doctrine might be a living thing in him," and that he might "desire to suffer His martyrdom, and mystically hang with Him on the same cross." If ever any man knew the meaning of "resisting unto blood, striving against sin," it was Savonarola.

Judged by the test that a great sermon is to make its hearers ready to fight and die for the faith, Savonarola was a supreme preacher. Moreover he is an illustration of my opening remarks in that he was a "timely" preacher, "a Christian opportunist" in the Pauline sense. His was an *adaptable* message, in the sense that he was not so inflexible in his views as not to modify his position under the stress of a consciousness of Divine coercion. This is, of course, most strikingly exemplified in his reluctant descent into the arena of politics; and his gradual perception, against all his prejudices, that a free Florence could only be won, and a Christian Florence could only be created, as the authority of the Word was acknowledged in the government of the city as well as in the administration of the Church. It is worth

your while to notice for how long a time
Savonarola's one ideal for the Church was
that she should excel in charity. It was re-
luctantly forced upon him, as it were, that
she must show herself the appointed guard-
ian of freedom and justice; and that to
quote his words, " It is the Lord's will that ye
should renew all things, that ye should wipe
away the past; so that nought may be left
of the old evil customs, evil laws, evil government." It was then that he cried out in
St. Mark's that he would not enter on affairs
of state " did I not deem it necessary for the
salvation of souls." " That *by all means* I
may save some," as Paul had expressed it.
He had come to see that any mundane reformation needs a higher inspiration than
motives of expediency. He challenged the
contemptuous dictum "that states cannot be
governed by Paternosters"; for the Lord's
Prayer is a fountain of all wisdom, social and
spiritual, and the men who have that prayer
in their hearts, are most likely to reform the
commonwealth to good purpose.

With his spirit newly-enkindled for the

great task, and his horizon of service widened, he laid down, and enforced it out of the Christian documents, that all power is derivative from the people; to use his own words, "that no man may receive any benefit save by the will of the whole people, who must have the sole right of creating magistrates and enacting laws." It was the new conviction in his soul that Divine sanction can be claimed for this political proposition, and that here lay the final safeguard against arbitrary power, and the ultimate guarantee of good citizenship, that changed the course of Savonarola's ministry, and clothed him for a while with the authority of social as well as moral leadership in Florence. I cannot take you through the details of what is, in the main, a glorious record of constitution-building, the abolition of unjust and arbitrary taxation, the levying of taxes only on real property, the establishment of courts of appeal, and above all the creation through the new order of government of a citizen unity, which, but for the revival of the base spirit of faction, would have saved Florence, and might have saved Italy, from many a disastrous chapter of history. Let any one whose artistic soul is wounded by the puritanical fanaticism that had vent in " the burning of the vanities," or any one whose calm modern mind shrinks from the recognition of weird visions as inspired leadership, or any one who reads something of cowardice into the awful decisions of the last fateful months, recognize if they can the astonishing practical sagacity of Savonarola's statesmanship, and his ultimate devotion to his ideals even through the bitterness of the stake and the cord, and the unspeakable moral anguish of being betrayed by the people of his love.

Let them remember, as I prefer to do, for final memory, the triumphant day when first the children of Florence were led from the folly and indecency of the Carnival into the great Church that they too might acknowledge and magnify the Theocracy which he believed was established as the government of the city. " Florence! Behold !" he cried to the vast multitude, as he lifted up the crucifix. " This is the lord of the universe,

and would fain be thine. Wilt thou have him
for thy King?" Thereupon all asserted in
a loud voice, and many with tears, crying,
"Long live Christ our King." No man has
ever failed in the Christian ministry who has
inspired a whole people, even for an hour, to
aspire to be subject to the sovereignty of
Christ.

From Savonarola to Calvin is only a few
years as we count time, but in the course of
a single generation Luther had arisen, and
with one great phrase—Justification by Faith
—had changed the politics of the greater
part of Europe. Luther is a fascinating personality and belongs, if ever man did, to the
romance of preaching. One may cherish un-
limited admiration for his war against a soul-
less and corrupt ecclesiasticism, while lamenting the fact that in the terrible period
of the Peasants' Revolt he did not see his
way clearly, and apply his Gospel principles
with equal consistency to secure freedom and
justice for those from whose ranks he himself had sprung. It is the more to be wondered at because Martin Luther was the most

human of beings, full of the milk of human kindness, devoted to wife and children, overflowing with laughter and humour, genial, quick-tempered, shrewd and passionately fond of music. On many sides of his character he was far more attractive and humane than the preacher of Geneva whose intense intellectual ministry I shall invite you to consider now. John Calvin is usually spoken of as the typical dogmatist; yet it was he who was responsible for the trenchant saying, " He is a fool who never has a doubt." Walter Bagehot objected to Voltaire's writings because, he said, nothing could possibly be quite so clear as Voltaire makes it. The man who does not realize the mystery of life and the universe explains nothing, and cannot really be an intellectual leader. We live in a queer world, but logic is not the key that unlocks the mystery of it. Calvin would have governed the world of the spirit by rule of logic, and the world of affairs by rule of thumb.

Neither experiment was a complete success. That he did such extraordinary things in the course of a life broken by ill-health and environed with every kind of danger and trial, is due to the fact that he himself was so much greater than his system. Let it be remembered that he completed the "Institutes" when he was twenty-four or twenty-five years of age, and probably began the task when he was not more than twenty-three. We are very wise at twenty-three, and see things much more clearly and definitely then than we do when we are twice the age. But I am one of Calvin's warmest admirers who believe with Mark Pattison that "his great merit lies in his comparative neglect of dogma," though I confess I sometimes gaze at the fifty-three octavo volumes of the Edinburgh edition of his collected theological works and vaguely wonder, if these represent a "comparative neglect of dogma," what would have happened to us if he had not neglected it. Let me, however, strike the key-note of Calvin's life and ministry by quoting Pattison's pregnant words: "Calvin seized the idea of reformation as a real renovation of character." While the German reformers were scholastically engaged in remodelling abstract metaphysical statements, Calvin had embraced the lofty idea of the Church of Christ as a society of regenerate men. The moral purification of humanity as the original idea of Christianity is the guiding idea of his system. The Communion of Saints is held together by a moral, not by a metaphysical, still less by a sacramental bond! That statement, I think, cannot be overthrown ; and it explains why John Calvin appears in Europe as a new apostle with a new message.

To pass from Savonarola to Calvin is to pass from a volcano sending forth torrents of molten lava to a well-contained and well-controlled furnace, whose fires are more effective because they are more disciplined. The volcanic eruptions on the other hand are far more picturesque, sensational and awe-inspiring. Calvin knew none of the paroxysms of the monk of Florence ; and in saying that I must not be understood to mean that the one type of ministry discredits the other ; but only that once again inspiration is following a law of adaptation. From Savonarola to

Calvin is from rhetoric to logic ; and nobody can read with intelligence this epoch of world history without realizing that Protestantism needed at the moment not rhetoric but reason. Moreover Protestantism had yet to show the world that it stood, not only for a more rational theology, and a simpler worship, but for a purer ethics and a sounder morality.

John Calvin went to Geneva to make a great experiment. He believed that a preacher of the Evangel might create and inspire a church, which should in turn become the instrument of freedom and righteousness in the civic life of the city. He had it in view throughout, to make Geneva central to the whole Protestant movement; and its citizenship so compact, united and resolved that the city would stand secure against all enemies. I would that every preacher setting out upon his life-work could have within him John Calvin's sense of destiny. Everybody knows how he resisted the call to Geneva, believing that his own work was in the study rather than in the market-place,

and how Farel stood over him and with prophetic vehemence pronounced a curse upon
his studies if he came not to the help of the
Lord in Geneva.   Calvin yielded to a resistless conviction of destiny and always felt that
the Almighty had shut him into Geneva and
locked the gates behind him.   Even when at
first the Genevans, alarmed at his moral
strictness, drove him forth from their midst,
with violence of hatred which shook Calvin's
sensitive soul to its centre, the Will and the
Sovereignty which were to become the foundation of his creed appointed his return, and
elected him to be the mouthpiece of God to the
city where, in the main, he ruled and taught
until his death at the age of fifty-four, and
lies buried in a grave which by his own wish
is marked by no stone, and is as unknown
to-day as the grave of Moses upon Nebo.

I am often compelled to contrast the sense
of destiny, or what we speak of as our "call,"
as it affected these fathers of ours and as it
affects ourselves. We speak almost invariably of a call to a church ; they spoke of a
call to a city. We are told all the circum-

stances that make a particular church a
desirable sphere of settlement ; its income, its
position, its social amenities, its agreeable
office-bearers and pewholders. Our re-
sponsibilty is to a special flock, whose sheep
are known by name, and duly enrolled as
such on the church books. But the destiny
of our forefathers was to the population of a
whole community. Their message was for a
city. Their responsibility was for the souls of
all people within the city gates, or the borders
of the township. They were conscious of
a pastoral relation between themselves and
the most obscure citizen of the poorest court
in the city. It was this fact that interested
them so keenly in the city problems—how
their community, little or large, was governed ;
the conditions of life that prevailed ; the
temptations to vice, luxury and crime that
lowered the standard of morals. They, the
preachers, were to take the field for public
righteousness as well as for religious truth.
I ask you to reflect what must be the effect
on preaching of this wider and deeper sense
of responsibility to one's fellows. I would

give anything in my power to get it back again for the modern ministry. A sense of responsibility to a church may be a very noble feeling; but a sense of destiny to a city, a town or a village is a far greater thing. Remember we are not Christ's ministers because we are called by a church; we are ministers of the people because we are called by Christ. It is the call of God we need to be conscious of in our hearts and in our ears. A minister in England or in America will talk about his call to the First Congregational Church, or to such and such a meeting-house; while the missionary more wisely inspired, or more greatly daring, will speak about his call to China or to Africa. It is the greatest thing in life when you can hear not only Christian voices calling you, but voices of those whose souls are dark or dead within them but who need all the more the message and the ministry that by God's grace you are able to give. John Calvin will achieve his greatest modern triumph, when he thus deepens and greatens the preacher's sense of destiny.

Students of Calvin's sermons and writings

will see for themselves how admirably the
instrument he employed was adapted to the
kind of constructive work he set out to do.
Members of congregations will note with relief that he evidently believed in short sermons; indeed he had no patience, as he said,
with a prolix style. Men have called him by
almost every depreciatory epithet, but, those
fifty-three octavo volumes notwithstanding,
nobody will truthfully call him "wordy."
Seldom will you read anywhere, discourses
with less of illustration or ornamentation
which are yet more penetrating and pertinent.
There are no chasings on the blade of his
sword. It is plain, keen steel, and with what
an edge! Calvin's style of address was, we are
told, somewhat slow and measured. For one
thing he was a martyr to asthma, and often
breathless in the pulpit and before the council.
It can be said of him, as it can be said of
very few, that he spoke literature. Strong,
stately, lucid, nervous, his sentences carry
you forward from point to point of his argument. Little wonder that the French school
books of to-day should point to Calvin as one

of the supreme masters and even makers of the
French language, and should describe his
style as an "admirable instrument of discourse
and of affairs."

It is remarkable that one who was so
scholarly in all his tastes should be the determined champion of extempore preaching.
Indeed he went so far as to declare that the
power of God could only pour itself forth in
extempore speech.   His criticism of the
Anglican Church, in his letter to Somerset,
was, " There is too little of *living preaching* in
your kingdom. . . . You fear that levity
and foolish imaginations might be the consequence of the introduction of a new system.
But all this must yield to the command of
Christ which orders the *preaching* of the
Gospel." He never ceased to insist that out
of the fullness of the heart the mouth must
speak ; and in one fine passage, with which
I may perhaps conclude this part of my lecture, he uses these memorable words, " It is
not said without reason that Jesus Christ
'shall smite the earth with the rod of His
mouth, and slay the wicked with the breath

of His lips.' This is the means by which the
Lord will bind and destroy all His enemies,
and hence the Gospel is called the Kingdom
of God. Although the edicts and laws therefore of princes are good auxiliaries for the
support of Christianity, God will make His
dominion known by the spiritual sword of
His Word, proclaimed by His ministers and
preachers." Whatever their faults may have
been these Reformation fathers believed absolutely in the power of the preachéd word.

Before I say a word of summary, let me
detain you very briefly before the portrait of
John Knox, who united to the statesmanship
of Calvin the fiery eloquence of Savonarola.
Perhaps I cannot introduce the man and his
mission better than in the words of the greatest of Scottish historians. " The whole fabric," writes Robertson, " which ignorance and
superstition had erected in times of darkness
began to totter ; and nothing was wanting to
complete its ruin but a daring and active
leader to direct the attack. Such was the
famous John Knox, who with better qualifications of learning, and more extensive views

than any of his predecessors in Scotland,
possessed a natural intrepidity of mind which
set him above fear." I agree with every
word of that last sentence unless it be the
word "natural." Knox insists that he was
by nature a coward; and personally I have
no difficulty in believing that "supernatural
intrepidity" would be the more truthful
phrase. It will interest you to observe that
he too was *driven* into his eventful work
against his own will and inclination. He,
like Calvin, was an example of a man worsted
in the fight against the Divine decree;
wrestling against the good angel of his destiny and being prevailed over to the endless
advantage of all subsequent generations.

After the martyrdom of the saintly Wish-
art, the Protestants in St. Andrews were resolved that Knox should take up the office of
preacher. He refused again and again.
Then John Rough, who afterwards perished
at the stake at Smithfield, dealt as faithfully
with Knox as Farel had done with Calvin,
charging him "to refuse not this holy vocation . . . as you look to avoid God's

heavy displeasure." Knox went out from the presence of John Rough to fight the battle out with his own soul, and "his countenance did sufficiently declare the grief and trouble of his heart." Finally he bowed to the declared Will, as a mighty tree bends before a mightier storm. Four months later the preacher of St. Andrews, the hope of the Reform movement in Scotland, was chained to a French galley, and for nineteen weary and desperate months tasted the French lash, labouring at the oar on the stormy north seas. But he had received his "call"; he had realized his "election," and no mutations of fortune could ever affect his sense of predestination to the task of delivering Scotland from superstition. It is just as well to meditate while we can, on the strength and stability which that old Calvinistic conception of God's sovereign purpose gave to the preachers who saw their own destiny in the light of it.

Sometimes, when I realize what trifling infirmities we allow to interrupt our appointed work for the Master, I reflect on such men as Knox with wholesome shame. With what ardour and zeal he wore himself out in the arduous campaign! Listen to this, of a certain James Melville, who had the eye and ear of a born reporter. "Of all the benefits I had that year [1571] was the coming of that most notable prophet and apostle of our nation, Mister John Knox, to St. Andrews. I heard him teach there the prophecies of Daniel, that summer and winter following. I had my pen and little book and took away sic things as I could comprehend. In the opening of his text he was moderate the space of half an hour; but when he entered to application he made me so to grue and tremble that I could not hold the pen to write." Mr. Melville goes on to tell us that at the time Knox was so ill and weak that he had to be assisted to the church and actually lifted into the pulpit, "where he behoved to lean at his first entrie," "but ere he was done with his sermon he was so active and vigorous that he was like to ding [beat] the pulpit into blads [pieces], and fly out of it." Such was the victory of the spirit over the flesh. If only young preachers knew to-day the power of a "mighty application" of their sermons, and the supreme art of training all their guns upon actual temptations and tendencies, upon actual sins and selfishnesses of their hearers, we should not have as much cause as we have, to lament the decline of pulpit influence and authority.

I have no time to dwell on the prowess of this heroic soul in holding out for God against a crafty hierarchy, a turbulent nobility, and the most dangerous Royalty in the world. The destiny of Scotland was in the scales; and under God, its freedom depended upon the fact that John Knox was no sentimental and effeminate champion of the new doctrine. Preachers have many temptations to be unfaithful to the truth; but John Knox had that to resist which had sapped the integrity, and compromised the virtue of some whom Scotland esteemed most loyal to the Evangelical faith. You remember Swinburne's lines on Mary Queen of Scots:

> " O diamond heart, unflawed and clear,
>   The whole world's gleaming jewel,
>   Was ever heart so deadly dear,
>   So cruel ! "

Mary was the cleverest, as well as the most beautiful of Rome's apologists. To the task of outmanœuvring and routing Knox and his army of peasant Protestants, she dedicated all her wit and all her graces. She flattered, she threatened, she cajoled ; she tried laughter, she tried tears. She could not believe that one man's conscience—and he of simple stock—could be proof against the wiles and the charms of the fairest queen in Christendom. But the one man she could not with all her craft hoodwink or bamboozle, was the Edinburgh preacher who never mistook her character, or was deceived by her artifice. Well might Mary exclaim in that famous interview, "I perceive that my subjects shall obey you and not me." History has it on record, that as John Knox passed out from the royal presence, the whisper went round, "He is not afraid," whereupon he replied, " with a reasonably merry countenance," " Wherefore should the pleasing face of a gentlewoman affray me ? I have looked upon the faces of many angry men and yet have not been affrayed beyond measure."

It is certain that the Christian minister who would be faithful to his trust, must yield neither to stern looks nor to soft speeches. Most of us can muster enough manhood, when we are put to it, to stand up against unworthy frowns. We have not always the courage that is proof against the seducing smiles of fashion, or wealth, or rank. Especially, we have not the insight of Knox, to whom external position was nothing, and the only reality that of the mind and soul. Good women are the most precious of all Heaven's gifts to the Church. We may well thank God for all there are, who devote the unique genius of their womanliness to the interests of faith and virtue. But there is need of just such a story as the one Scotland cherishes, to teach us all, betimes, that everything is not necessarily angelic that looks like it ; and that the most difficult, delicate and dangerous of all controversies is, when Truth finds itself in opposition to Error, Superstition and Vice arrayed in the most attractive and alluring guise, and when the whisper of siren voices may seduce even the best-

intentioned voyager, from the integrity of his
course.

I have put these three preaching ministries
together, because they are supreme examples
of the power which the man of the Gospel
can exercise in shaping the civic and national life of free peoples. They were all
preachers of a puritan spirit. It is probable
they made mistakes, and ever since have
been the objects of the slighting criticisms
of those, who have made few mistakes because they have attempted few enterprises.
What the world owes to the example of
Savonarola, to the constructive thinking of
Calvin, and to the statesmanship of Knox,
can never be told. Thanks to them, and to
others whom I cannot stay to commemorate,
we have come to hold that the ideal State is
as much a fruit of the Gospel as the ideal
Church. Any errors they may have committed, are far more than compensated for,
by the priceless witness which they bore to
the sovereignty of Christ over all mundane
affairs. Of course they were buffeted and
bruised, as all must be who descend into the

arena.   Of course they tasted to the full the reproaches, calumnies, and cruelties of those who repudiate the authority of the Christian preacher, save in matters of abstract faith alone.   But I do not imagine that if they had their lives to live over again, and knew quite well the sufferings and disappointments that awaited them, they would choose differently.   For there is, as Carlyle said, no victory but by battle.   There is no crown but by the cross.   There is no triumph for the preacher save as he pledges himself to the kingdom of God, and makes himself the willing instrument of that resistless Will which shall yet, in obedience to our Master's prayer, be done *on earth* as it is done in heaven.

LECTURE VI

THE FOUNDERS OF FREEDOM:
JOHN ROBINSON AND THE PIL-
GRIM FATHERS

LECTURE VI

THE FOUNDERS OF FREEDOM:
JOHN ROBINSON AND THE
PILGRIM FATHERS

THE Gospel is more than a great faith; it is a great adventure. Its news is so good that it must be carried everywhere at all hazards. The most thrilling pages in Christian history describe the enterprise of the Evangel.

When a leading English Review, that has a reputation for cynicism, some time ago described the missionary movement, its cynicism gave way to genuine enthusiasm. " They have kept alive at the heart of a selfish and materialized culture," it declared of our missionaries, " a genuine heroic tradition " ; and went on to say that there were few families of note in England that had not made some contribution to the army of missionary martyrs, and that "all the ends of the earth are hallowed by their graves." No man can

read such records without emotion and
pride. There is no history to compare with
it, nor ever can be. It is something to
realize in these days that unselfishness can
devise and achieve greater things than selfishness ever can. We all know that science
and commerce have inspired expeditions
which have filled the world with admiration ;
but the simple truth is, that the adventures
inspired by the disinterestedness of Christian
evangelists, have thrown all other enterprises
into the shade.

There have been many types of missionary
preachers and missionary adventures. Much
that is best in America to-day, derives from a
pilgrim race. In the words of Mr. Lowell,
they crossed the Atlantic " to plant their idea
in virgin soil." They may not have looked
romantic. Shovel hats and long black
cloaks do not compare in picturesqueness
with the embroidered raiment of the cavalier
heroes of Vandyck. Yet these men and
women, so prim and demure of outward
aspect, set forth on the most astonishing
of adventures, reading their destiny west-

ward in the heaven of their ideals, and by
the good hand of God prospering them, sow-
ing the world with free commonwealths. A
clever modern novelist has invented for us
the title, " The Belovéd Vagabond." It
might have stood for a description of the
Mayflower. You may read on a tomb in
that spellbound burial-place at Plymouth,
part of an address delivered by a preacher
whose body rests beneath. He describes his
associates as " my beloved adventurers."
That great writer, Professor Seeley, says,
" Religion alone can turn emigration into
exodus." Who shall define or describe the
mystic determining impulse that drove the
Pilgrims into the wild, to make a home for
faith and freedom? Had they any pre-
science of the greatness of the goal? Did
they, too, see an Abrahamic vision of a seed
as the stars innumerable, for those who would
go forth not knowing whither, but content
to follow the gleam? Did they say, when
the winds of heaven filled their sails and
bare them far from friends and fatherland,
"the spirit driveth us into the wilderness " ?

Were they all equally clear that the Will of God was with them, and that in the Book of Destiny their names were written as the humble pioneers of a new world and a new order? Were all hearts westward and forward, and all minds constant in their resolve? Did none nourish a treacherous appetite for the flesh-pots of Europe, murmur at the discouragements of the journey,

" Nor cast one longing lingering look behind ? "

How gladly would we know more than we do, or ever can, of the details of that golden romance, which surely, outside the pages of the New Testament, is the greatest story in the world !

Savonarola ruled Florence, Calvin ruled Geneva, John Knox ruled the realm of Scotland. Each in measure asserted the authority of Christ over a turbulent and sometimes rebellious population. Their difficulty was that they were compelled to put new wine into old bottles, until new bottles could be wrought and shaped for the new wine. The Pilgrim Fathers would have a new bottle for their new wine. They demanded a free commonwealth suited to their free ideals of worship, and of citizenship. They could not be content to graft their new branch on the old decayed stock, where it must be overshadowed by all the other branches that bare fruit of so doubtful a flavour. For the most part they were business people who found Leyden a tolerable town to thrive in. But their religion made them restless. The Promised Land was in their hearts. The more John Robinson preached to them of the primitive church, and the destiny of the kingdom, the less they were satisfied with the compromise-society which alone was possible to them where they were. We may perhaps be thankful that the result of faithful and real preaching is not always, as in the case of John Robinson, that the congregation arise and flee. But I confess I always suspect my own preaching of weakness if it does not make many young people uncomfortable, and compel them to become missionaries of the ideal, even at some considerable sacrifice. "Will you be content," argued

John Robinson in effect, "to go down to your graves with your witness undelivered, and your bravest hopes unattempted? Or will you risk something, nay everything, to translate your theories of Christian freedom into a veritable free society?" The problem of Savonarola, Calvin, Knox, was whether the preachéd word was powerful enough to transform and convert an old order. The problem of John Robinson and the Pilgrims, was whether the preachéd word was powerful enough to create and establish a new one.

Before I come to a somewhat closer study of the man and his ideals who inspired one of the world's most momentous enterprises by his preaching, I shall ask you to spare a thought for that revival of preaching which marked the heroic age, in which the mind of England was turned permanently Protestant. I say the *mind* of England, for no serious student believes that we were made Protestant by the domestic vagaries of Henry VIII. We were made Protestant by an open Bible, and its prophets. One lesson had been taught by the ballads of Chaucer, and the

visions of Piers Plowman, and was reënforced
afterwards by the tracts of Martin Marprelate,
that *to win the ear of the people you must talk
their language.* To popularize the Reformation and its new religious ideals, it was necessary that preachers should arise who thought
in the vernacular, and who seasoned their
speech with the salt of such homely words
and phrases, as made Tyndale's Bible understanded not only by the college-bred, but by
the smith at the anvil, and the labourer behind the plough.

When Hugh Latimer began to teach the
new doctrine from St. Paul's Cross, every
London apprentice knew and relished his
message. After all, is not this one of the
signs of a new Pentecost, " We did hear tell
in our own tongue the wonderful works of
God "? There is a saying of Jesus that we
shall all do well to lay to heart: "What I
tell you in secret, that publish ye on the
housetop." Christianity is every man's religion ; and therefore can be translated without loss into the language of the street. It
is a religion for the open air. It is a religion

that does not suffer by being brought home
to the conscience and reason of simple folk.
It is susceptible of learned philosophical
statement, I doubt not, satisfying to the
greatest and profoundest thinkers, but John
Ruskin once said, with the touch of exaggera-
tion characteristic of him, " What a little child
cannot understand of Christianity, nobody
else need try to." The essential Protestant
faith captured the ear and the heart of six-
teenth-century London, through the pithy
pregnant Saxon speech of Latimer, with his
command of laughter and tears.

He presented the citizen in the street with
a plain man's religion. He spoke it as
simply, I say it with reverence, as the Saviour
spoke to the peasants in the fields of Judea,
or the fishermen by the Galilean lakes. He
did not so much appeal to the theologically-
trained mind; and he certainly did not appeal to any sense of ecclesiastical authority.
He appealed to common sense; he appealed
to the instincts of the multitude. He appealed to their love of justice and of humanity. There never was a more human

being than Hugh Latimer.   The people well know the men who love them, believe in them, and understand them.   The sheep hear the voice of the true shepherd.   London has always been a city with much that is artificial and materialistic in its complicated cosmopolitan life ; and no one ever held the key of its affections who was not a true man. Latimer's preaching is oratory stripped of all that is meretricious, and oratory that is not sterilized by conventionality.   No timid, stilted pulpiteer, who has never learned that grace is more than grammar, and that to win your hearers, you may break every pulpit convention that was ever designed by a sleek respectability to keep our volcanic Gospel within the bonds of decency and order, will ever capture the soul of a great city, or speak with a voice that will ring in the hearts of a free people.   And if Latimer knew the secret, another knew it who is worthy to be named with him—that passionate pilgrim of the Puritanism which was only Latimer's Protestantism become logical and thorough—I mean John Penry.   They burned

Latimer at Oxford, and hanged Penry on a gibbet in the Old Kent Road; but not till these men and others like-minded had set England on fire. For one thing, they had shed their blood for freedom of thought and freedom of speech, and no martyr has ever died for those sacred principles in vain. The preacher's very existence was at stake in the controversy, whether religion was to consist of prayers and offices rendered in a foreign tongue, or the truths which free men were to think and speak in their own free speech. In the former system the prophet has no place; in the latter system he is the most precious possession of his age.

I hope I shall not weary you by insistence on this point; but the tendency of theology to become an esoteric philosophy, full of technical terms understanded only by the experts, has the inevitable effect that its professors and teachers lose touch with life. Always the preacher must be a man of his time. His business is to restate the eternal message of salvation in the terms of to-day. Chaste and cultured archaisms are pleasant

to the palate of the scholar ; but the Gospel
is for the people, and we need more than
anything else, men of the people who know
their needs and their thoughts, and can make
the Evangel, what it eternally is, the property
and heritage of the simple and the poor.
Some of you will recall, by way of illustration, the scathing satires of Erasmus on the
scholastic theologians and preachers who, in
his time, made it their business to cultivate a
reputation for erudition and profundity, by
talking in words that the vulgar could not
understand.   This is a specimen which Erasmus gives of the teaching of these inflated
doctrinaires.   " They say that ' person ' does
not signify relation of origin, but duplex negation of communicability *in genere*, that is,
it connotes something positive, and is a noun
of the first instance, not the second.   They
say the persons of the Divine Nature exist
reciprocally by circumincession, and circumincession is when a thing subsists really in
something else which is really distinct, by
the mutual assistance of presentiality in the
same essence."   After reading two or three

lines of that kind of thing, you feel as if you were in a lunatic asylum. Do you wonder that men and women sickened and wearied of it? And do you wonder that the Reformation preachers brought a veritable new revelation to the world when they read out to the common people such great simple words as these, " I am the Way and the Truth and the Life ; no man cometh unto the Father but by Me " ? If Tyndale had done nothing else by his translation of the Bible he had taught us for all time that there is no more dignified and majestic diction than the simple speech of the common people.

I cannot explain to you just why it is, that the true prophet is always a master of simple speech, but it is certain that no man can speak home to the hearts of his fellow-men without it. Inasmuch as the Reformation was a return to the natural and to the human from the artificial and the scholastic, it did more than change the world's history, it revived the order of prophets, and it created a literature. From Hugh Latimer and John Penry, to Daniel Defoe and John Bunyan, you

can read the influence of the Reformation in
bringing religion back to life, and making it
the inspiration of the common people.

After all, it was but natural that the Puritan
preacher with his love of reality, should be
impatient of the mere tricks and artifices bor-
rowed from the demagogue.   The Richard
Bernard who was only " almost persuaded "
to become a pilgrim, and just missed immortality thereby, dealt out wholesome warnings
to young preachers in his book entitled " The
Faithful Shepherd."   How he satirizes those
brethren who, as Mr. Spurgeon used to say,
"mistake perspiration for inspiration," and
try to produce an impression by violence
which could not be produced by the weight
of their argument!   Some forward ones, he
declares, are "moved to violent motions as
casting abroad of their arms, smiting on the
pulpit, lifting themselves up, and again suddenly stamping down."   Others "through
too great feare and bashfulness which causeth
hemmings, spittings, rubbing the browes,
lifting up of the shoulders, nodding of the
head, taking often hold of the cloake or gown,

fiddling with the fingers upon the breast but-
tons, stroaking of the beard and such-like
toies." There is sound sense as well as
humour, in this attempt to put us on our
guard against ridiculous and meaningless
nervous gestures which distract and annoy
the most indulgent of our hearers, and add
nothing to our power. It is always easier in
this matter to enforce the truth by precept
than by practice ; but nothing is more certain than that the man who has learned early
the right modulation of the voice, and to be
content with those simple gestures which are
natural and dignified, has mastered what is
fundamental to the art of pulpit oratory.

That this was no chance judgment of
some isolated Puritan divine, but one common to all in that generation, may be further
gathered from an excellent passage in one of
John Robinson's forceful writings. "As a
woman, over-curiously trimmed, is to be sus-
pected, so is a speech. And indeed he
that goes about by eloquence, without firm
ground of reason to persuade, goes about to
deceive. As some are large in speech out of

abundance of matter and upon due consideration, so the most multiply words either from
weakness or vanity.   Some excuse their
tediousness, saying that they cannot speak
shorter, which is all one as if they said that
they have unbridled tongues and inordinate
passions setting them a-work.   I have been
many times drawn so dry, that I could not
well speak any longer for want of matter ;
but I could ever speak as short as I would."
I ask you, could the thing be better put?
Could there be a better comparison than this
of a highly-rhetorical speech or sermon to "a
woman, over-curiously trimmed " ?   Have we
not had to listen to many discourses where
you could not see the dress for the trimmings?
It may be impossible to lay down any canons
of good taste in this matter, but I shall venture to submit to you, that the Puritan frugal-
ity of illustration and adornment, is far more
effective than the prodigality and even profligacy of quotation and ornament which is
sometimes popular among us to-day, and
which may dazzle, but does not really subdue
and persuade an audience.

Nevertheless, you are not to suppose that John Robinson could not estimate the worth and value of apposite and pointed illustration. Dr. John Brown has borne testimony to the wealth of his reading, the catholicity of his range of knowledge. He has discovered quotations from Plato, Aristotle, Herodotus, Thales, Cicero, Terence, Pliny, Plutarch, Seneca, Epictetus and Suetonius among the classics ; among the Fathers, from Ignatius, Tertullian, Cyprian, Ambrose, Augustine, Gregory Nazienzen, Lactantius, Jerome, Basil and Eusebius ; among later writers, from Bernard, Anselm, Scaliger, Beza, Erasmus and Melancthon, as well as his own contemporaries. This renowned preacher and scholar, who was to inspire men and women to attempt and achieve one of the most heroic tasks in history, was a man steeped in literature, who had wrestled in his study with great themes, who had sat at the feet of men of mind of all schools and generations, whose culture was as catholic as his sympathies were wide, and who yet, as Tennyson says, "wore his weight of learning lightly as a flower," and never lost touch with his fellows, or gave up to academic ambition what was meant for mankind. Had it been otherwise, he might have become a walking encyclopædia, but never the mainspring of that gallant adventure which planted a free church on a free soil.

The more I study the personality and the preaching of John Robinson, the less I wonder at the spirit and exploits of the community whose members owed everything to his inspiration. Under the strongest temptations to intolerance, he maintained a generous temper and a broad Christian outlook. He was immovably firm in the maintenance of principles, but even his controversial utterances are distinguished by a large charity that lifts him above his time. And I cannot be wrong in arguing, that his ministry bears the marks upon it of the influence of his church, which was almost alone among the separatist communities of the time in its freedom from unworthy partisanship, and the frictions and bickerings which are the fruits of jealousy and pedantry. I imagine John

Robinson would have found it difficult to decide whether his people owed most to his preaching, or his preaching owed most to his people. One has the feeling that such a church would have made almost any preacher eloquent ; yet again, one is driven to conclude that such a preacher would have created a true church out of almost any material. The fact of the matter is, of course, that the atmosphere of faith and prayer does make good preaching inevitable, whereas the attitude of suspicion and criticism will " freeze the genial current of the soul," and give to any earnest and spiritual minister a sense of labouring at the oar to no purpose.

It is not possible to leave out of account that many preachers are called to preach to the worldly, the unbelieving, the indifferent and the hostile ; and we should be contradicting some of the most glorious facts in Christian history, if we did not recognize that God does not leave His witnesses alone when they go forth on His errands, no matter how difficult the journey. But it is almost impossible to separate John Robinson from the church he loved so deeply, and which loved him with equal intensity and constancy. He was just one of the members of the body, deriving health and power from his vital relation to all the rest, and communicating his own life and strength to them. When he spoke to this outside world, when he put pen to paper, when he became a champion in controversy, and a defender of his faith and people, it was not he alone who spoke. The whole church seemed to become eloquent in and through him. Equally impressive is it, that the church members to whom he gave his blessing, and a double portion of his spirit, seemed to reproduce his faith, courage and charity when far from his presence.

Leagues of tempestuous Atlantic waters never separated people and pastor in ideal or in fellowship. Still the mystic spiritual tie held. Still they thought together, and prayed together, and aspired together, and wrought together. It was as if he, their pastor, were present at every council meeting, was a guest in every cabin, prayed at the bedside of the dying, joined the hands of the newly-wed,

and committed those who died in Christ to
their last resting place in the forest. Of all
the blows that fell one by one upon that
struggling Pilgrim community in the bitter
heroic days, when death and famine seemed
their most familiar acquaintances, the most
crushing and heart-breaking was the news of
the death of their beloved pastor ; and every
soul in Plymouth colony felt as if his father
had fallen, and sorrowed most of all, that they
should see his face no more.

We have got to believe more than we do,
in this sacred coöperation of preacher and
people. We shall have no ideal preachers in
the pulpit, unless and until we have ideal
hearers in the pew. For conquests that will
startle and awaken the world, the need will
always be for prophet spirits who are sus-
tained and illuminated by their contact with
a society of consecrated souls. It is all very
well to lecture students for the ministry on
the vocation and equipment of the preacher,
or on the ideal of his calling, but in sober
truth, such lectures ought from time to time
to be delivered to the officers and members

of churches and congregations. *They* make
or mar the ministry. They encourage or
discourage the preacher. They make it possible for him to be at his best, and impossible for his arrows to miss the mark. They
create the atmosphere in which faith can live,
and doubt cannot. They arm him for unseen
conflicts, and protect him by their prayers
from insidious attacks on his moral integrity.
Moreover, it is they who multiply his message,
translate it into living fact and deed, and so
give power and effect to his ministry. Let
it never be forgotten that modern America
sprang out of the ideal relation between a
pastor and a church ; a man of God and a
people of God.

Let it never be forgotten that the problem
was thought out in church meeting, and the
enterprise planned and adopted within the
atmosphere of a Christian assembly. It was
there, while men and women pleaded for
light, and for faith to walk in it, that the
spirit of illumination was vouchsafed, under
whose gracious guidance the yoke became
easy and the burden light. Together, while

the prophet-leader saw his vision, and the
people kindled to it, they became equal to
the sacrifice, and confident of the Will and
the Way. I cannot analyze how much of
those faithful discourses that will stir men's
souls to the end of time, was due to the rapt
and resolute faces of simple heroes and heroines that were upturned to meet his gaze, and
how much of their exaltation and enthusiasm
was due to their contact with a soul in which
indubitably dwelt Divine insight and fire ;
I only know that their sublime *coöperation*
made the westward track of the *Mayflower*
plain, and wrote the new Book of Genesis in
the Bible of human destiny.

Forgive me if I linger lovingly on these
familiar scenes, so big with fate, and so
weighty with instruction. The preacher who
has not pondered over these origins of New
England's history, must blame himself if he
has missed much inspiration for his own
work. The part played by Moses in the days
of the Jewish exodus towards the Land of
Promise is not one wit more notable or significant than the part played by John Robin-

son in the exodus that ended in this land of
promise.   I might spare a moment or two
for examples of his genius in the employment
of rare and suggestive texts of Scripture, and
his skill in turning out-of-the-way incidents
in Bible narratives to profitable account.
There are many seemingly desert places in
Scripture, that a preacher who knows his
Bible, can make to blossom like the rose.
Not that there was any strained ingenuity
about John Robinson's way with texts.   But
who would forget that text out of the Book
of Samuel from which he preached on the
special day set apart for inquiring the mind
of the spirit as to this enterprise, "And
David's men said unto him, Behold we be
afraid here in Judah ; how much more then
if we come to Keilah against the armies of
the Philistines ?   Then David inquired of the
Lord yet again.   And the Lord answered
him and said, Arise, go down to Keilah ; for
I will deliver the Philistines into thine hand."
Among all your New England towns to-day,
I wonder if there is one named Keilah ; and
if not, whether it is too late to supply the

omission ? Unless all reports lie, there are
still enough Philistines left to justify the experiment.

Then on the ever-memorable day when he
preached to the Pilgrims for the last time, the
sermon that has become an imperishable
legacy for all forward souls, he found his text
in the Book of Ezra, "I proclaimed a fast
there at the river Ahava that we might afflict
ourselves before our God, to seek of Him a
right way for us, and for our little ones, and
for all our substance." Think how these
felicitous words must have accomplished
their purpose, which was to provoke to new
fervour of prayer and faith those who at the
crisis of their fate still needed to be assured
that theirs was a God-prompted and God-
guided enterprise. Often, when I study the
preaching of our fathers, I am impressed by
the fact that they knew their Bibles better
than we do. They had less of the light of
criticism, but they had, I think, notwithstanding, a more exact knowledge of Holy
Writ. To-day this great territory of Scripture is like a modern continent ; extreme and

unhealthy congestion at certain well-known centres, and vast tracts of country uncultivated and unknown. How many of those listening to me have been led against the "Philistines at Keilah," or have heard "a fast proclaimed at the river Ahava"?

Perhaps we flatter ourselves that if we had part and lot in so wonderful a movement we, too, should be moved to search the Scriptures, and to uncover some of their hidden gems of price. But that is to harbour an undeveloped imagination. Every hour of assembly is a time big with destiny. Every Sunday men and women go forth from the tryst with God to face measureless possibilities. Suppose that you and I, who have the unspeakable privilege of interpreting the book of life, realized that the men and women we are addressing are as capable of disinterested sacrifices and noble exploits as their progenitors at Leyden; and that before a week is out some of them may have launched their *Mayflower*, and embraced a God-given adventure, with what emotion would our speech to them be charged? If we fail, it is because we do not see the possibilities latent in what we call an "ordinary congregation." No assembling of ourselves together to meet with Christ can ever be "ordinary." That is only a fashion of speech. We say sometimes, " It was just an ordinary service." If we have ceased to expect extraordinary manifestations of God's power, and revelations of His will—that our young men should see visions and our old men dream dreams—why is it? It was just as possible that your fathers at Leyden should say "Yes" or "No" to the beckoning hand of their divine destiny, as that we should accept or reject the higher Will for our own. There was no single element present at their fateful assembly in their Leyden meeting-house, that may not be present at any hour of worship in these days, and in the land of their adoption. All that is necessary for us to repeat their enterprises and achievements, is soul enough to believe in God's will and to surrender to His leadership.

I am impressed by the fact, that the last picture of their beloved minister which the Pilgrims carried with them to their promised

land, was the one so simply and vividly
described by the historian of their enterprise.
" The tide—which stays for no man—calling
them away, that were thus loth to depart,
their Reverend Pastor, falling down on his
knees, and they all with him, with watery
cheeks, commended them with most fervent
prayers unto the Lord and His blessing."
I suspect that we have all at times felt what
we call the burden of extempore prayer.
But I am certain that the soul of the prophet
is most surely and powerfully revealed in his
prayers. To speak to men of God is a high
privilege. There is perhaps one higher : it
is to speak to God for men. I do not doubt
that many a great saying of John Robinson
lingered in the memories of his pilgrim flock,
and was recalled under the pine-trees and
behind the stockades in their new settlement.

But assuredly the most sacred recollection
of all, was of his tender and loving interces-
sions on their behalf ; and they came to feel
that the greatest moments in their lives, were
those ever-memorable ones when that proph-
et-spirit talked with God, and they saw

heaven open, and heard things scarce law-
ful for man to hear. God forgive us that
our pulpit prayers tend to become so formal,
and even unreal! For this is the sublimest
office the minister of the Kingdom is called
to fulfill. It is out of such spirit of communion and sacred intercourse with Deity
that the pilgrim ambition is born, and the
pilgrim vow sealed and ratified. Nay, I go
further. It is in our prayers that our real
ideals and hopes for our people are revealed.
If we have great aspirations for them; if in
our personal desire we destine them to sacrificial service; if we so love them as to cherish for them the glory and honour of the
God-dedicated and forward-moving life, they
will make the discovery in our prayers. For
it is in our prayers that the deeps of the soul
are uncovered, and the passionate yearnings
of the true minister for his people make themselves known. That is a great adjective
which Scripture applies to the fervent prayers
of a good man. They are "energizing."
They charge receptive souls with new and
sublime forces. They reëstablish broken or

imperfect connections with the source of Divine power. They baptize the waiting, willing, listening heart with new vitality. They " energize "—dare I say " electrify " ?— the mind. Who can doubt that those who knelt around their spiritual father at Delfthaven, with the rickety ship *Speedwell* lying near as if to remind them of the perils and discomforts of their adventure, were braced and strengthened and " energized " for their deathless task by the fervent applications of that man of God? Let no preacher among us fail to realize the power of inspiration that may communicate itself through his sermons to his congregation ; but least of all let him forget that the final stimulus to deeds of faith and devotion will be felt and known by his people in the supreme hour of fervent and energizing prayer.

I must ask you to spare one thought for a feature of the famous expedition on which perhaps we do not often dwell. No minister went with them ; that is, no ordained preacher and pastor. Apart from the fragrant memory of their former leader's ministry, they were dependent on what we sometimes speak of as a "layman's" service. I would like to press Elder Brewster's example upon you, as another and unanswerable argument why we should not deprive ourselves, as we do, of the spiritual wealth of men and women in our churches who have not devoted themselves to the formal ministry, but whose thought and experience would enrich our corporate life. Would to God that all the Lord's servants were prophets! When shall we get away from the paralyzing misconception that a man of affairs is thereby incapacitated from being a spiritual leader? I make no doubt that the meditations of Elder Brewster were all the wiser and nobler that he had many public anxieties to bear, and responsibilities to carry. It ought to be forever symbolical of New England, that the religious spirit was united to the spirit of practical citizenship in him who, unordained of man, assumed spiritual leadership within the pilgrim theocracy.

So the preaching of the Word, and the higher Idealism, resulted in the founding of a new world "dedicated to the proposition," as Lincoln would say, that Christ's will is the only worthy and wholesome law for a state. To recover that ideal we need a new race of prophets—seers of inspired vision like John Robinson, statesmen of spiritual experience and moral stature like Brewster. How the Pilgrim church created the Pilgrim state ; how it drew up as Mr. Bancroft says, "the first instrument conferring equal civil and religious rights on every member of the commonwealth " ; how it sought to do the will of God on earth is matter of history. Imperishable as that history is, it is of little worth for the world of to-morrow in comparison with the necessity that her new preachers and spiritual leaders should "highly resolve," that they will bring to the stupendous task of creating yet another "new world" a double portion of the spirit of their sires—the same faith, fortitude and sacred adventure, a like endurance in the teeth of danger, suffering and death, and " an equal temper of heroic hearts."

LECTURE VII

THE PASSION OF EVANGELISM: WESLEY AND WHITEFIELD

LECTURE VII

THE PASSION OF EVANGELISM:
WESLEY AND WHITEFIELD

THE problem of the Preacher as evangelist is one of which we are all bound to think, and on which history has much to teach. I shall begin by agreeing that we make far too sharp a division between a ministry that is educational, and a ministry that is evangelistic; and too marked a distinction between a morning service for edifying the saints, and an evening service for evangelizing the sinners. There seems to be no adequate reason why people should take their minds to church in the forenoon, and their souls in the evening. If occasionally more soul were put into the morning sermon, and more mind into the evening sermon, we might improve the quality of the saints and make the conversion of the sinners more permanent. But when that

is said, I shall proceed to state **my main**
proposition with all the force I can command—
that it is time all Christian preachers equipped
themselves more definitely for evangelistic
work, and refused to allow the most vital
part of their aggressive policy to be under-
taken for them by an order of preachers however able and devoted who have to be called
in for the purpose like consulting physicians
at a crisis.   The ministry that is not an evangelistic ministry is not in the full sense a
Christian ministry, for we cannot obey our
Lord's command and leave His Divine appeal unuttered to those who are heedless and
unresponsive.

But it is equally certain that evangelism,
rightly understood, is not as simple a matter
as it seems.   It is the greatest mistake in the
world to imagine that defects in education
are a qualification for evangelism ; or that, to
put it in another way, such an absence of real
culture as would disqualify a man for the full
work of the ministry might rank as an endowment for his work as an evangelist.   I
rate the work of evangelism far higher than

that. It is work that demands the best brains we possess; and no training can be too thorough, and no reading too wide for the minister whose aim it is to be to bring the irreligious and the indifferent on to the side of Christ and the Kingdom. We can never forget that it was Paul, the most accomplished and erudite of the apostles, whose soul was fired most with a passion for evangelism before which all the old racial barriers went down like a bowing wall and a tottering fence.

Does anybody suppose that he would have been better fitted for his apostolic work if he had never sat at the feet of Gamaliel? So far from lamenting the catholicity of his culture, we know how much depended upon his ability to become as a Greek to win the Greeks, and as a Roman to win the Romans. I am not prepared to argue that the result of learning is always to widen the sympathies; and that learned men are invariably the most human and versatile of beings. Experience hardly warrants so satisfactory a generalization, and Carlyle's old friend " Dry-as-dust," "with loads of learned lumber in his head," does exist even outside novels like "Middlemarch." Indeed, the notorious fact that many profound scholars have been men of narrow sympathies and pedantic opinions, has been responsible for the fear, that one may still hear expressed, lest promising young preachers should be ruined at college by being made too bookish and scholastic. But Paul's example is decisive as to the value, for the work of evangelism, of that generous culture which frankly confesses the debt it owes to Jew and Roman, Greek and Barbarian,—a confession which, in itself, is more than half the victory over those disabling prejudices which prevent a missionary from getting on terms with his audience. It is surely not too much to say that, humanly speaking, no untrained and uncultured man could have done Paul's work among conditions so diverse. The Church of to-day needs to ponder deeply on this fact, that it was the man of most massive intellect and most varied scholarship, who was the first great Christian evangelist.

No one will claim for St. Francis of Assisi

the rank of a scholar ; but his education was good as the standard of the time was, and there are no evidences of weakness in that charming intellect which he carried with him through his spiritual pilgrimage to the Italian peasantry. But as to his namesake, Francis de Xavier, there are no deductions to be made. He who was to wear his life out in romantic evangelistic journeying through lands that were at that time the *Ultima Thule* of travel, was educated in the University of Paris, became a lecturer in the Aristotelian philosophy, and might have successfully aspired to almost any position in that academic world, so brilliant were his intellectual talents. One cannot have all the gifts ; and even Xavier confesses in his letters that he had no skill in languages, which was the reason why his work had to be done through the difficult medium of an interpreter, and why the legend arose that his deficiencies in this respect were conveniently made good by the gift of tongues. No grammars and dictionaries were available in the strange lands of his voluntary exile ; and, had

they been, he had no time for their study.
But to a hero of his spirit there was less embarrassment in this deficiency than most men
would have suffered. For he had within him
the universal language of sympathy and faith,
which was the secret of his amazing conquests.

Even in these modern days there is something staggering in the bare record of his
phenomenal travels. Fever and peril, by land
and sea, had no terrors for him. From
Portugal to Mozambique and on to Goa;
from Goa to Travancore; from Travancore to
Ceylon; from Ceylon to Malacca; from
Malacca to Japan; from Japan back again to
India, and through that last desperate fight
for a foothold in China; we watch this fiery
and intrepid evangelist, whose powerful mind
was undaunted by the social, moral and
religious difficulties which the life of the
Orient presented. There are always some
people who argue that men of the first rank
in intellectual power are thrown away on
evangelistic missions, either to the depraved
of their own land, or to the habitations of

heathenism. As they watch the academic career of a Henry Martyn till he fulfills the highest ambition of a mathematical scholar at Cambridge University, wins the University prize for Latin composition, is appointed a fellow of his college, and then dedicates his talents to the mission field, they cry in protest, "To what purpose is this waste?" But they do not tell us by what means, or in what career, those brilliant parts of Henry Martyn might better have been unified and concentrated and employed, for the welfare of humanity.

Think of him as Sir James Stephen describes him in his Cambridge days, and before his life decision had been taken. The passage is a famous one : "a man born to love with ardour and to hate with vehemence ; amorous, irascible, ambitious and vain ; without one torpid nerve about him ; aiming at universal excellence in science, in literature, in conversation, in horsemanship and even in dress ; not without some gay fancies, but more prone to austere and melancholy thoughts ; patient of the most toilsome inquiries, though

not wooing philosophy for her own sake;
animated by the poetical temperament, though
unvisited by any poetical inspiration ; eager
for enterprise, though thinking meanly of
the reward to which the adventurous aspire ;
uniting in himself, though as yet unable to
concentrate and to harmonize them, many
keen desires, many high powers, and much
constitutional dejection—the chaotic materials
of a great character." Chaotic materials indeed ! How the vision came to Henry
Martyn, in the light of which this chaos was
resolved into order and harmony, and how
henceforth he saw his way, and could say
with the apostle, " This one thing I do," is the
story of his conversion, and his self-dedica-
tion to the work of an evangelist. To those
whose thoughts are engrossed with secular
ambitions, his was a lost life, and he himself
the mere victim of a fanaticism that laid waste
his powers. But to all who understand what
are the real honours to be won on this earth,
and the permanent foundations of fame, Henry
Martyn's disinterested devotion, and sacrificial labours, belong to those records which

make us proud of our humanity. The
beautiful tribute might be paid to him which
is engraved on the cenotaph of John Howard
the prison reformer, in St. Paul's Cathedral,
that " he followed an open but unfrequented
pathway to immortality."   There were, doubtless, many easier and pleasanter pathways
open to him ; but his feet followed where his
heart and his reason led the way. He had
reached what, I often think, is the most profound conviction possible to us, and one which
can only be entertained by an intellect that is
powerful enough to penetrate to that reality
which lies beneath the outward shows of
things—the conviction expressed in a passage
in his journal written about the natives on his
first landing in India, " I feel that they are my
brethren in the flesh, precisely on a level
with myself." You may put that saying of
his side by side with David Livingstone's
confession that, after living among and for
the native Africans, he forgot that they were
black and remembered only that they were
fellow-mortals. I repeat, that it does not require a powerful mind to perceive the external

differences between one race and another, but it does require an absolutely just and strong reason to discern the fundamental unity of humanity, and to live in the consciousness of *that*, rather than of any outward distinctions, whether of colour, class or creed. This, indeed, I should be disposed to regard as the most indispensable endowment of the evangelist. The converted prize-fighter, in John Masefield's vivid poem, cries out :

> " I thought that Christ had given me birth
> To brother all the sons of earth."

And surely we may with confidence contend, that this is the purpose and effect of the new birth. The new spirit that is created thereby is one of brotherhood to all the sons of earth without distinction. This is not the language of sentimentalism. It is, once again, a " glory of the lighted mind." It is the fruit of the spirit of justice and equity new-born within the God-surrendered soul. If I were alone in the opinion I should still maintain that the supreme proof of Henry Martyn's intellectual greatness is not to be found in his

New Testament translated into Hindustani,
or the Book of Psalms translated into Persian,
but rather in the absolute fraternity of spirit
which inspired his labours among the beggars
of Cawnpore, and the unshaken constancy of
purpose which held him faithful through his
final painful wanderings, until fever-wasted
and shattered by disease, he sank, at the age
of thirty-two, into his lonely grave at Tokat.
Such was the passion of evangelism which
exalted and mastered Henry Martyn, so that
the young brow of a famous Cambridge
scholar wears, to-day, the aureole of a modern
saint ; and so that Lord Macaulay was moved
to write the well-known lines of him :

> " In manhood's early bloom
> The Christian hero found a pagan tomb ;
> Religion, sorrowing o'er her favourite son,
> Points to the glorious trophies which he won.
> Eternal trophies, not with slaughter red,
> Not stained with tears by hopeless captives shed ;
> But trophies of the Cross."

But surely we may say that outside the
apostolic era, the greatest evangelistic move-

ment was the one that changed the face of England, and gave birth to the new era of missionary expansion and adventure. The breath that filled the sails of the good ship *Duff*—the first distinctively missionary ship that ever sailed the ocean—was in reality that mystic rushing mighty wind which swept over the lifeless soul of England at the great Pentecostal season of the evangelical Revival. The new missionary enterprise was the witness to the reality of this rebirth of the Church. The satisfying proof that the Lord was visiting His people was, that the unknown heathen of Tahiti were seen to be not only as needy, but as worthy of sacrificial service, as their brethren in the neglected villages and city-slums of England. The regenerate churches of Christ, in my own country, could not close their eyes to the vision of a perishing humanity, but fervently believed that Christ had, indeed, given them birth

" To brother all the sons of earth."

Yet if ever evangelism had plausible excuse to offer for concentration, and a narrow-

ing of the area of service, it was at that
memorable time. Something that sounded
perilously like common-sense took up its
parable, and pleaded that, until the work of
Christianization was complete at home, it
was mere waste of good money and valuable
lives to evangelize the far islands of the
Pacific. Could Henry Nott find no sphere
of work as a city missionary in the East end
of London, that he must hazard everything for the Tahitian cannibals ? It was, at
bottom, the old heresy that would have
chained Paul to Jerusalem, and imprisoned
Christianity within the narrow limits of
Palestine. The old patriotism of the *Jewish*
prophet might have persisted, but the new
patriotism of the Christian prophet must assuredly have perished. What I have called
the epic of world-conquest, would have been
no more than a poor attenuated apology for
a great poem. The plain fact is, that Christianity cannot fly either a national or a racial
flag. It is world-empire or nothing. This
is its Romance. The Cross must claim its
sway over all continents, islands and oceans,

or its glory is departed.   That is why evangelism is so essential in any true interpretation of our religion.   It sounds the universal
note.   It levels, in faith, all barriers.   It has
a regenerate imagination.   It is fired by the
patriotism of Humanity.   The passion for
souls is its mainspring.   Material space is as
nothing.   The soil of England or America is
of no more consequence in the sight of the
Son of Man than the soil of Tahiti, Central
Africa or Labrador.   Evangelism means the
love of man as man.   That is why its results
are so mighty.   That is why the most obstinate prejudices melt away before it.   That is
why, when churches grow cold and self-
centered, and lose the evangelistic spirit,
straightway those bigotries reappear, and the
cruel divisive walls that sever man from his
fellow-man are rebuilt.   Evangelism, and
the spirit it represents, is the secret of the
unity of humanity.   Within its breast lie the
spiritual forces that are to conquer the proud
and bitter antagonisms of great empires and
nations, safeguard the rights and liberties of
the weak, and create the just and equitable

spirit which is the best guarantee of world-peace and world-progress.

I am still insistent that, for the noblest form of evangelism, God wills the dedication of the finest intellectual powers, because I am arguing that the policy of evangelism is demanded and justified by the highest reason. We all remember that the evangelical Revival which saved England morally, spiritually and politically was born at Oxford, which has not only been as Matthew Arnold said, "The home of lost causes and forsaken beliefs," but the birthplace of many a reformation to which mankind owes much. Wise men are always watchful of those centres of thought where the representatives of the coming generation are facing the issues of life. But I do not know that the wisest observers of that day indulged in any radiant prophecies as to the future influence of the much-ridiculed members of the Holy Club, or spared more than a passing thought for two ardent young men, John Wesley and George Whitefield, who were associates in the society stigmatized by that name.

To be quite frank, John Wesley, as a youth, was not a very lovable person; and Whitefield's perfervid and dramatic nature had vent in extravagances calculated, rather to alienate than to attract, the average University undergraduate. But all the same, through the petty persecutions and even violent controversies in which they were involved, the honours of war were all with those who could not be satisfied by the arid and ambitionless faith, which did duty for Christianity over well-nigh the whole area of so-called Christian England. They knew that if God was a fact, and Christ's Gospel a reality, then the existing church in England was a caricature and a farce. They felt, moreover, that to be the ministers of Christianity meant to be in the grip of a resistless Power, servants of an inerrant Will, whose Sovereignty could not be satisfied with anything less than the surrender of the whole being. They faced the claims of Christ, even as they appropriated His promises, with unshrinking trust; and the result was, that when the time came, they were found to be endowed with a vision of the Kingdom such as had not been conferred by apostolic hands on any of their clerical contemporaries. The name and tradition of George Whitefield are perhaps especially dear to me; but I should not be true to my own convictions if I did not confess that John Wesley, as his was the finer intellect, was the more powerful evangelist so far as permanent results were concerned. There are tests by which this may be judged, apart altogether from the obvious statistical ones. George Whitefield, to the end of his life, never realized what human slavery meant, nor saw any inconsistency in offering spiritual redemption to those whose physical servitude he was unwilling to end. Wesley's keener and stronger mind searched the slave system to its foundations, and unhesitatingly and passionately condemned it. Yet Whitefield's temperament was far more naturally sympathetic and tender than Wesley's. Where he fell short was in intellectual power; and that shortcoming was responsible for the lack of real human statesmanship, which spelled failure to secure the full results of his unparallelled labours.

I know all that can fairly be alleged against John Wesley's strength on the intellectual side, by reason of the vein of superstition from which he was by no means free, and his lamentable misjudgment of the American case, at the time of the War of Independence. It is well to know that our heroes are so vulnerable, as there is the less temptation to dehumanize them by a doctrine of infallibility. But one thing there is about John Wesley which every careful student of his career, and especially of his preaching career, must observe—that he was never satisfied to persevere in any course which he could not justify to his own reason; and that again and again he changed his views against all his traditions and prejudices because he could not defend an attitude of obscurantism or conservatism. It is characteristic of him that when he first meditated taking orders in the Church of England, he was involved in serious difficulties because of the Calvinism of the articles, and the " excluding clauses" of the Athanasian Creed. As everybody knows, his objection to White-field's programme of field-preaching sprang out of his intimated stiff prejudice in favour of the existing conventions that governed public worship and the preaching of the Gospel.

But he could not resist the argument of the Sermon on the Mount ; and he saw that apostolic practice was of far more importance and authority than ecclesiastical conventions, which could neither be defended by Scripture nor by common-sense. Let us remember not only his limitations, but all from which he emancipated himself. Let us remember that by temperament he was an aristocrat ; and that his affinities were rather academic than democratic. Remember his scholarly endowments ; that he and his brother Charles were accustomed to converse in Latin to the end of their lifetime. Remember his passionate and pathetic devotion to the church in which he was ordained, and his concern to be her faithful son, subject to all reasonable authority. Then recall how, in spite of the past, and in spite of himself, he was taught by slow experience that for the work of Evangelism he must sound the universal note. " I am a priest of the Church Universal," he claims ; and again utters the memorable words, " The world is my parish." The fascination of John Wesley's life is in the gradual achievement of full spiritual liberty, and emancipation from the trammels of ecclesiastical convention, as his spirit is by degrees illuminated in actual contact with his fellows, and through a deep experience of the laws and methods of salvation.

If that argument is not conceded, I should have to make appeal to his sermons ; and I should do it with all confidence. As evangelistic discourses they are most significant and most surprising. The evidences of a mind steeped in classical culture and keenly alive to the thought of his time, abound on almost every page. Every perusal of them leaves me wondering, what it was in them, that pierced the consciences of the most hardened sinners to the quick. There is nothing sensational in this evangelism. There is plain dealing.   There is much practical, sensible and serious exhortation as to the sins that corrupt men's lives and harden their hearts.   Of rhetorical fireworks there is not a trace.   We are less impressed by the vehemence than by the calm strength of them. Yet certain it is, that when this man preached, the world knew that the hour of battle had sounded.   Those scenes of fury, which belong now to English history, and in which Wesley's life was again and again in peril, are the tribute to the power of his message. If he had been arguing for a verdict before a society of learned men, he could hardly have reasoned more closely, or employed more classical illustrations.   From which fact surely one lesson of supreme value may be drawn. The evangelist, on whom all Hell is let loose, has yet no need to let his mission down, or condescend to base and unworthy methods of attack or of appeal.   Such means do not really and permanently *tell*.   Even as Wesley was singularly fine and pure in controversy when he was being assailed by a multitude of scurrilous pens, and pelted with gutter-epithets, so, also, in the warfare which he waged with error and evil in almost every market-place in the land, he was content to use the Gospel weapons of Truth and Love, and as the smoke cleared from the battle-field it was seen that he and his forces were in possession of the best strategical positions.

I grant you that, often enough, in the face of the granite indifference and apathy with which the preacher is confronted, the temptation to try the earthquake, the hurricane and the explosion, and to mistrust the still small voice, is very natural and very great. But sensationalism does not win Wesley's victories, nor ever can. At the long last, the conquests of the Cross are seen to have been won by the old-fashioned weapons of persuasion, patience, sacrifice, courage and overwhelming sympathy, joined to that sagacity or common-sense which in Wesley amounted to genius, and that was the secret of the extraordinary organization which, more than a century after his death, holds together for worship and service millions upon millions of Christian people.

If I do not attempt any description of the complementary but contrasted work of George Whitefield, it is because the characteristics of his famous oratory have been described by so many writers. We may accept the almost universal verdict that for dramatic and declamatory power he had no rival in his own age, and no superior in any age. Doubtless it was true, as Mr. Lecky observes, that he had a narrow range of ideas ; but it is also true, as the same historian reminds us, that his genius and disposition suited him to " the position of a roving evangelist," that he was " adapted for the boisterous vicissitudes of the itinerant life," that he excelled in impassioned religious appeals—which seem never to have lost their force or their freshness though repeated hundreds of times —that his preaching " combined almost the highest perfection of acting with the most burning fervour of conviction," that " his gestures were faultless in their beauty and propriety," that he had "a large command of vivid, homely and picturesque English, and an extraordinary measure of the tact which enables a practiced orator to adapt himself to the character and disposition of his audience," and finally that he possessed "a contagious fervour of enthusiasm which like a resistless torrent bore down every obstacle." All this is very true, if very trite. His art was so perfect that he could invest "tawdry and even ludicrous strokes" of rhetoric with extraordinary power; and it should be remembered that he set it before him, on his own admission, to rouse the passions to the highest point, especially the passions of love, hope and fear.

All these characteristics belong to the externals of his ministry, and it may well be urged that without them his open-air campaign must have failed in its effect. Let us remember how Whitefield viewed the opportunity. To him, England was the theatre of a great struggle, a fierce and terrible war, which must be fought out with every perfection of armament by the Christian host if the day was not to be lost, and the soul of a people destroyed forever. He did not fit himself out with rhetoric and dramatic skill merely to entertain the populace. "By all means he must save men." If the arts of oratory were necessary that he might storm the consciences of the democracy, then in what better cause could he practice them? We may choose to recall that men and women of the finest taste and highest consequence were avowedly his admirers; that Garrick, David Hume, Benjamin Franklin, Lord Chesterfield and the Countess of Huntingdon came under the spell of his marvellous eloquence; but it is no more than justice to remember, at the same time, that it was not for these that he equipped himself with so much labour, and pursued his methods with so much courage. It was for the miners and the puddlers and the weavers; the masses of neglected and ignorant artisans and field labourers, to whom clergymen and ministers had ceased to appeal, and for whom in all the land there existed no passionate sympathy until George Whitefield arose, and spoke to them in a voice often choked with tears of death in sin, and life in Christ.

It is Whitefield who so pointedly raises, for

the student of oratory and its permanent effects, the problem of emotional preaching. Mr. Lecky tells us that "no talent is naturally more ephemeral than popular oratory." He does not go on to tell us that no talent has produced such mighty results. The man who can kindle the multitude, recreate faith in a worldly age, and inspire the ideals of a whole people does more than all the authors, artists and statesmen put together. We, in England, know perfectly well how the moral power was generated which in the early years of the nineteenth century swept the slave-trade from the Empire, cleansed the prisons, multiplied the schools, revolutionized the constitution, and established a large measure of religious equality. All these reforms, and many others, were the product of the new religious life of the common people. Whitefield may have believed, or thought that he believed, that Christianity aims at gathering out of a lost world an elect, fit but few; but it was his practice and example rather than his dogma that prevailed, and his practice was to make appeal not to the few

but to the masses, believing that the power
of Christ over them is beyond all calculation ;
and the results, if they discredited his Calvinism, abundantly justified his evangelism.

There are three points of great practical
value which I ought to press home upon you
before I close. The first concerns the *art* of
popular preaching ; the second concerns the
place in evangelism of theological formulas ;
and the third concerns the " call " of the
masses. On each of these I should like to
say a very few words.

(1) Popular preaching has come to have
a bad name among us. We are tempted to
pride ourselves on preaching that is unpopu-
lar, and to assume that the best test of good
preaching is that it should empty churches
rather than fill them. The man who draws
and holds the crowd must, we presume, be
a superficial preacher, while the man who reduces his audience, like Gideon's army, to a
small and high-souled elect, is like a farmer
who has successfully operated a milk-sepa-
rator, and has retained only the pure and
rich cream. This operation on the part of a

minister is by no means uncommon, and is usually assumed to be due to profound thinking. I suggest that we have come to the time when we may wisely reconsider this problem. The common people heard our Lord gladly, and it is difficult to pay compliments to ourselves, if they do not care to hear us at all. I submit to you that in our reaction against a frothy emotionalism, we have gone to the extreme of impoverishing our preaching of the human touch, and by so doing we have lost our power over the human heart.

When I read our Lord's infinitely moving lament over Jerusalem, or His impassioned indignation against religious hyprocrisy, I marvel that we can ever imagine Christian preaching to be admirable that is not deeply penetrated with emotion. I am told that this sort of advice does violence to our modern temperament and attitude of mind. To-day we are all for self-control. We think a man is a fool to "let himself go." Enthusiasm is at a discount; scepticism is in the ascendant. I am told that love has given

place to the science of eugenics ; and that
in the well-regulated modern world, when
the Romanticist and the Poet have been
suppressed in the interest of pure science,
emotion and imagination will have no place.
If this be so, our Revelation is still to the wise,
foolishness ; but it does not follow we are to
surrender to any so-called scientific school.
At any rate, if my protest were the last word
ever to be said in a Lyman Beecher lecture
in favour of " human preaching " and the
cultivation of the art of popular oratory, I
would venture to say it.   You have every
chord of the human heart to play on.   Surely
the art of eliciting their music is worthy of
your study and cultivation.   Men and
women, after all their history and education,
are still human beings, compounded of
laughter and tears, sunshine and shadow.
Humanity is still, as it has always been,
capable of the heights of heroism, and the
depths of shame.   Not one of the elemental
human passions has been eradicated by all
our philosophies.   No process of evolution
has carried us, or ever will, beyond their grip.

Life and death are just as poignant experiences as in the early days of our race ; and if our refinements have done anything for us, they have made us more sensitive and not more stoical. We may, of course, ignore these facts, and assume that those to whom we preach are above all things engrossed with metaphysics, and have an inward craving for the critical probability that there were two Isaiahs. But if that is our attitude we have much to learn. Nobody ought ever to go into a pulpit who can think and talk about sin and salvation, and the Cross of Christ, which is for all true men the symbol of hope and service, without profound emotion and passion.

I recognize that for the business of reading moral essays, disquisitions on ethics, or treatises on movements in theology, but little equipment in oratory is needed. Oratory indeed is unthinkable apart from the inspiration of some great human theme. When the preacher's soul is blessed with real vision, and the hand of the Lord his God is upon him, he will be conscious of profound unrest until he can deliver his soul to those multitudes in the valley of decision, to whom his message represents the way of life and liberty. Do not misunderstand me. The order of preaching friars must always be a catholic one ; and there is room in it for the man of quiet, thoughtful spirit who delivers to a devoted flock his meditations on the Gospel. But I like that phrase of the apostle of Patmos, descriptive of his own experience— " He *carried me away* in the spirit." We cannot always be in the same mood, nor if it were possible would it be well. But surely this is one of our noblest capacities—this of being transported out of ourselves by the vision of God, and of His will, " carried away " by the rush of emotion, enthusiasm and imagination to that lofty standpoint where we greet the dawn of the Day of Christ's Kingdom on earth ; and watch the Holy City, New Jerusalem, descending out of heaven from God. That is why I lay stress to-day upon the highest possibilities of preaching. We are always being told that this is a materialistic age ; that modern industrialism has no soul ; that as our machines grow more human, the men who make them grow more mechanical. It is true. And for that very reason we want Poetry back again, and Art, and Music, and, above all, the Prophet who is the supreme interpreter of the spiritual.

When I look at the famous portraits of Whitefield, and conceive him as he faces the multitude under God's sky, with the heavens for sounding-board, the hillsides for meeting-house, and some rude boulder for pulpit ; as his splendid energy expresses itself in the fold and sweep of his robes, and his passion for souls in his kindled countenance, his flashing eye, and the tender solemn tones of his voice, I feel as if this is the one thing to pray for—that God will raise up a new race of genuine orators of the evangel, who without any unworthy artifices will shake men's souls and thrill their hearts.

(2) In the second place I am bound very briefly to express my belief that theological formulas will matter comparatively little in the new evangelism. My reason for saying this

is an historical one. The two men who together were responsible for the Evangelical
Revival were representatives of two contrasted schools of theology, which all the
praiseworthy efforts of their successors have
not been able wholly to reconcile. Whitefield affirmed with immense conviction what
Wesley decried with equal strenuousness.
There never has been in the history of
theological controversy, a deluge of pam-
phlets so virulent, and so scurrilous as those
with which their partisans assailed one another. You might easily have supposed
that these antagonistic schools of theologians
would have neutralized one another, or, at
least, minimized the general effect of their
mutual labours. But it was not so. And
the reason is, of course, that in the mercy of
God the blunders of our finite minds are not
permitted to prevent His Word from having
free course and being glorified. It is not
creeds that bring the breath of life back to
exhausted souls, but faith.

That is not to say of course that crude and
unworthy teaching about God or man may

not produce painful reaction of an intellectual sort. This that I am saying is no plea for slipshod and shallow thinking. But just as the most profound and wise theology may utterly fail to inspire the hearer to virtue and to faith, apart from men of soul and fire to believe it and to preach it; so a theology that is greatly inferior in intellectual strength may nevertheless be more than compensated for by a preacher whose heart God hath touched. It is faith, faith, faith, that conquers the world. The life of God is the strength of the saints; and it is the same divine life in Calvin and in Wesley, in St. Francis of Assisi and John Knox, in Jonathan Edwards and Henry Ward Beecher. In man's fight for life as a spiritual being the mystic breath of the Divine Spirit is more than all our formulas.

(3)   Lastly, evangelism recognizes the call of the masses. Explorers tell us that there is a resistless power in "the lure of the wild." They tell us that after a taste of it they soon weary of our tame conventional civilization ; and prefer all the risks and hardships and

perils of the wild to the monotony of our unambitious and routine existence. There is a very true parallel between the life of the explorer and the life of the evangelist. The true evangelist listens to the call of the wild —that raw, untamed, passionate human nature that is a yet unknown and uncultivated soil but that has all the virgin possibilities of limitless fertility. I do not think our Lord had no feeling of reverence for the Temple and the synagogue, and those who were in sincere association with these, but I do think His soul responded to the call of the wild,— the churchless multitude, neglected, outcast, uncultured, waiting only for the ploughshare and the seed to become glorious with the harvests of God. To-day we may well thank God, as I most humbly do, for our churches. They form the base of operations for every good and great campaign. But the campaign must not be restricted to their boundaries. The campaign is for the lands beyond the frontiers. The Church is still the homeland to all the soldiers. Its patriotism fires us. The warmth and joy of its hearth glow

in our hearts when we are out on the great
adventure. Perhaps we never learn to love
it until we come to know at first hand the
meaning of that unhallowed secularity where
its atmosphere does not extend. Let every
preacher resolve he will be churchman and
evangelist in one. The call of the Church,
and the call of the wild are both to be heard,
I think, in the soul of every true ambassador
of Christ. We may not love Jerusalem less ;
but the song of the pioneer must be ever in
our hearts and on our lips, "They shall build
the old wastes—the ancient wilds,—they
shall raise up the former desolations, they
shall repair the waste cities,—the civilizations
run to waste,—the desolations of many generations."

LECTURE VIII

THE ROMANCE OF MODERN PREACHING

LECTURE VIII

THE ROMANCE OF MODERN PREACHING

THE danger of lectures that deal mainly with the past, is lest the final impression should be left, that our own time is in the nature of an anti-climax to the illustrious generations we have been passing in review; that the great gates leading into the spacious lands of opportunity are all closed, and that nothing remains to us but some shabby and petty doors giving upon meagre and uninteresting fields. Some critics speak as if there would have been no romantic or heroic chapters in Christian history, but for the grim and forbidding figures of the bigot and the tyrant, with all their sinister apparatus of torture and death. Sermons have been preached in celebration of the funeral of bigotry; though bigotry takes a deal of burying, and has singular gifts of resurrection after its obsequies have been ostensibly performed.   Nevertheless, the arm of the persecuter has been so far shortened that we no longer see the blackened stake in the market-place ; and the instruments by which heretics were put to the question, are regarded as the evil evidence of an intolerance and an inhumanity that we have outgrown.   Now and then, even in those days, our heroes and heroines suffer death at the hands of those who know not what they do. Still the graves of the self-exiled evangelists of the Cross multiply in fever-haunted lands ; and lonely saints make brotherhood with lepers, or burn out for Christ among savages on remote islands or in the dark African interior.   But apart altogether from the fascination of incidents such as these, which lend themselves to picturesque descriptions, I am determined to persuade you in this closing lecture that the work of the preacher in modern times remains as romantic and dramatic as ever.

The question is whether we believe in the mission of the Christian prophet as Wagner, let us say, believed in the mission of Music, or G. F. Watts in the mission of Art. Of the latter, as you may remember, a modern poet wrote these fine lines by way of epitaph :

" He knew her destined mission, dared to hail
    The place assigned her in the heavenly plan,
  Reader of visions hid behind the veil;
    Elect interpreter of God to man."

That is no more than to say that George Frederick Watts was an artist with the soul of a prophet ; and that with his canvas for pulpit he preached, and will preach as long as his pictures last, sermons that prove him to be verily an "elect interpreter of God to man." In whatever medium he works, the man who has the soul of the prophet will fulfill the same mission. His will be the skill to read the "visions hid behind the veil." He will keep alive the faith and the knowledge that there is a world of reality behind the veil. Thus he will fulfill his destiny to deliver his generation from the dark influences of a materialistic science, and to restore Faith, Hope and Love as the guiding and govern-ing realities of life. Let me repeat what I have said before—that if the preacher is doomed to disappear as rationalism and materialism triumph, then the poet, the artist and the musician will disappear in like manner at the same time and for the same reason.

But now let us ask ourselves, what it is about our high calling that gives it a perennial fascination and glory? For the only thing that can kill preaching is, that we should lose the sense of its majesty and unique authority. The first thing that I would say is, that *preaching can never lose its place so long as the mystery and wonder of the human spirit remain.* For we are dealing with that which is the source of all the amazing interest of life. Man is a creature mystically elect to strange conflicts and adventures of mind and soul. He stands alone in God's august creation, in that he knows the exaltation of spiritual vision, and the humiliation of remorse for sin. He has inexplicable beatitudes, and as inexplicable sorrows. His mysterious history is blood-stained and tragic; but it is lighted everywhere with almost incredible heroism. Robert Louis Stevenson would persuade us that personality is dual, and that every soul among us is half angel and half devil. Certain it is that underneath purely worldly exteriors, dwell unsuspected philanthropies and benevolences. Sordid and callous speculators whose ambition seems to be to rig markets, or inflate and depress shares at will, have pure affections and holy memories lying detached from their daily business existence, like a ring of lilies around some foul morass. Conversely, some men and women to whom the world bows down in respect and esteem, carry with them the memory of secret sins, the consequences of which all their zeal cannot overtake.

The homes of the poor are the dwelling-places of romance. Not a tenement staircase that does not echo to the feet of Love and Hope, and all the attendant train of ministering angels ; while Jealousy, Envy and Despair and their evil brood are to be met there likewise. I venture to say it is the experience of all those who visit sympathetically among the poor, that they rarely come across any house where, in some corner or other, they do not distinguish the footprints of the

Son of Man ; He makes the place of His feet glorious. The more we know of life the more we discover what compensations and alleviations are due to the divine capacities of the human spirit. The child of poverty sits in some corner of the ill-furnished room. She is reading the story of " Ivanhoe," and following breathlessly the adventures of the stainless Knight. For a while she is not in that wretched home at all. For her the lists are set, and the lances conched, and the horses caparisoned. To her knights bow, and courtiers bend, and grand ladies smile. Forgotten are hunger and hardship and the dreary outlook. She too is " carried away in the spirit." How our hearts would leap if we could really read all that lies behind the faces that confront us so enigmatically on the Sunday. What of their faiths and their doubts ; their ambitions and dissatisfactions ; their yearnings and wistfulness—and all covered with so impenetrable a mask that except in rare cases of confidence their nearest and dearest friends are not permitted to penetrate beneath the surface to the intimacy of their real life? Yet suddenly, at any moment, that may happen which will break up all reserve, and bring the strong man to you groping blindly for light, pleading for help and comfort like a little child. For the hour cometh to all when it is Jesus Christ or nothing; and all the dollars in America cannot pay the passage-money across the inevitable sea.

We preachers live always in the conscious presence of the supreme mysteries. We deal with men and women, many of whom are afraid to face them. It is our business to know what doubt and grief and death can do; it is our business to prove what, given the Gospel, doubt and grief and death cannot do. But I should delude you if I were to suggest, that this sacred task is to any of us at any time an easy one. The first incident in my own ministry that I vividly remember, was connected with a bright young girl who on her twenty-first birthday was enjoying a picnic-party on the Thames. Her lover went to the side of the launch to get a camp-stool for a friend, tripped and fell into

the river and was drowned before her eyes.
In a moment life's happiest pageantry turned
to darkest tragedy. Well do I remember
being asked to go and see this stricken one,
and I shall never forget pacing up and down
the street outside the house with the drawn
blinds, trying to muster up courage to go in.
Why had no one told me that the Christian
ministry was like this ? I can see now in the
dark room the white marble face as of one
changed to stone ; I can see her holding out
hands to me for faith, when I was bankrupt
of my own !

It is easy to stand up in a pulpit, and to a
listening crowd preach the truth of Christianity ; but the preacher has to say something
that will count for faith and comfort, when
souls are tortured by sorrow almost to the
last agony. Have you taken a walk in the
spring-time, and felt disposed to take your
shoes from off your feet before the miracle of
a flowering thorn ? What a little while ago
was a bunch of black stems, with forbidding
spikes and thorns, is now a glorious mass of
gay flowers, shedding fragrance all around.

What a Divine touch it is that can make the thorn to flower, and express its inner life in such rare grace and scent ! Have we a like Divine secret to turn the thorns of life to beauty and sweetness ? Let no man venture into the ministry without that knowledge. It is the veritable key that opens the dungeon of Despair.

The men who interest and fascinate us most are they who illustrate the wonder of the human spirit, and teach us preachers with what potentialities we have to deal. Man's uniqueness in the universe lies in the wrestlings that are not with flesh and blood, the struggle for existence that is not physical but spiritual, the conflicts with principalities and powers that are invisible but real. Bunyan suffered much from external persecutions, but no one who has read his autobiography can possibly believe that his physical sufferings in prison, were at all comparable to his agony of mind and spirit, when doubts threatened the faith that was the very breath of life to him. Cromwell knew the pains and hardships of the battle-field and the sorrows that scorn and hatred can inflict ; but his greatest conflicts were in the spirit, and his hardest fights were with himself and his own passionate temper and disposition. Luther tasted to the full the cup of tribulation and anxiety ; but you must read his commentaries to discover that the fiercest war he waged was not with the Church of Rome, but with the treachery of his own heart and will.

You will ask yourselves whether such men as these are alone in their mysterious strife, or whether it is in some degree appointed to us all. What means this exercise of the mind and soul in the problems of faith ? Have we not problems enough of a more practical sort ? Why is mankind thus tormented with spiritual anxieties ? Why, indeed, if the sceptic philosophy of to-day be true which reduces all faith to illusion, and spiritual vision to the agitation of certain nerve-centres ! By that interpretation, the noblest chapters in biography are the record of incredible folly and stupendous tragedy. These agonies of the higher life, that mark the progress of man with drops of bloody sweat, that distinguish all his pilgrimage through the valley of humiliation and the shadow of death—what are they but the proofs of the divinity of the human spirit, and its struggles in the grip of the consciousness of its destiny, and of the sublime imperative of faith ?

The second thing I would say to you is, that *amid all changes of thought and phrase the wonder of conversion remains,* to be the supreme joy and glory of the preacher. A congregation gathered in the name of Christ, and prepared by prayer for that message which is the supreme call to life, is to me a momentous assembly.   It is the arena where God and Self fight out stupendous duels. It furnishes an atmosphere in which anything may happen. At any moment Saul may come to his crisis and the new Paul be born. For our Gospel is not the survival of the fit ; but the revival of the unfit.   And here in the society of Christ, those divine forces are leagued and focussed which decide the destinies of individuals, and even of nations. Within that congregation men are being braced up for big renunciations, and sacrificial enterprises. The voice from the pulpit is the ally of the trembling and even fainting soul, that is at the point of giving up the battle for virtue and righteousness. Lame consciences struggle to their feet again. Nerveless wills are stiffened and strengthened. It is as if a wave of pure ozone passed over the breathers of some exhausted air. You feel the stir of hope. Feeble and enervated spirits drink the elixir of life, and are conscious of recovery of tone and health. The tonic air from the hills of God works its miracle of rejuvenation, and faith is born again.

There are so many sorts of conversion. It is conversion when the faithless soul believes ; and it is conversion when a little faith becomes a larger faith. It is conversion when bad men become good men ; and it is conversion when good men become better men. It is conversion when the hands that hang down are lifted up; and when the lame and erring feet are turned back into the way. It is conversion when the business standards of the world are exchanged for

higher and more human standards; and
when the decision to do the brave and
honourable thing forces itself within a
worldly mind. While the preacher is at
work, any one and all of these changes may
take place. If he believes in his business,
and in the coöperation of the Divine Spirit,
he expects great events to happen. No
service can ever fall to the dead level of the
commonplace. Every hour spent within that
atmosphere of faith, beneath the spell of
Christ's presence and personality, is charged
with mystic feeling.

My own personal belief is that we do not
realize, as we might, the possibility of sudden
conversions. When we read the story of
Henry Barrowe, who was one of the founders
of modern Congregationalism, passing down
the Strand in a wild mood, and entering a
church to scoff, and remaining to pray, passing as Lord Bacon said "at one leap" from
a libertine youth to " preciseness of conduct,"
we do not doubt the story, and all Barrowe's
after life until the day of his martyrdom was
a witness to its reality. But who can ex-

plain that magic "leap" of the spirit from dissoluteness to uprightness, and from the darkness of doubt to the light of faith? Was such an experience possible only in days of intellectual renaissance, or moral revival? Is it too much to hope that the assembly of praying and believing souls, and the witness of God's ambassador, may still lay a sacred spell upon the soul? In the biography of one, who even in our tolerant nineteenth century suffered imprisonment in England for conscience' sake, and wrote in his prison a history of America, it is told how in his careless youth he was arrested by the preacher's message; and when, at the close of the sermon, the congregation began to sing the quaint old hymn

" If Jesus is yours, you have a true friend;
His goodness endures the same to the end.
Though pleasures may tarry and comforts decline
He cannot miscarry, His aid is divine,"

"such was the emotion I experienced," he says, "that I cried out before them all—'Jesus is mine!'" That experience was one on which he never went back; and the Presence he realized then and there lighted in later days his prison cell.

But my question is whether we have lost the capacity to force careless and worldly hearers to review their life? Possibly if your children of to-day were suddenly to rise up and make use of some such exclamation as I have indicated, you would call in the family physician, and ask him whether he thought it was the liver or the nerves. The very possibility of those searching spiritual experiences which shake life to its centre seems so remote to most of us, that it can hardly be said to come within our consciousness. Yet there is not one of us who does not know that, historically, these sudden illuminations have often marked the birth-hour of new eras of human progress. I have never thought that John Wesley was a very likely subject for abrupt mental or spiritual change; for in many ways he was compact of ecclesiastical prejudices. Yet at that little Moravian room in Aldersgate Street, when suddenly he became conscious of that strange inward warmth and light of which he wrote so simply and nobly, Mr. Lecky tells us a new chapter in English history was opened, and, I may add, one of the most fruitful of all chapters.

Those ministers, if such there be, who do not believe in these swift crises in man's intellectual and spiritual life, are those who are still the victims of the false view of time, and who have not yet realized with what freight of significance these flying minutes may be laden. This belongs to the romance of our opportunity, that so much destiny may be crowded into so brief an occasion. The surgeon may make careful preparations, but how deft and swift is the critical work when the cataract has at last to be removed from the eye. The miracle of spiritual sight-giving is swifter still. The flash of a thought— who can measure the duration of it? The glow of a new-born affection—who can estimate the length of time of its origin? The outreach of the soul in faith towards its Saviour—by what principles can you judge if it be swift or slow? All that we know is that God can do His most amazing work on human souls with a rapidity that even to think of dazzles us. We have ceased to repeat, and perhaps to believe, the old lines :

> "Between the saddle and the ground
> I mercy sought, and mercy found."

But no transition of thought will ever destroy the inherent truth and beauty of the memorable sentence in Hawthorne's "Blithedale Romance," describing the suicide of Zenobia, "the fleeting moment after Zenobia sank into the dark pool—when her breath was gone, and her soul at her lips—was as long, in its capacity of God's infinite forgiveness, as the lifetime of the world."

Again, and in the same connection, let me remind you that the preacher is always living through the romance of the spring-tide. The spring-tide is the time of mystic changes; when unpromising and unattractive seeds and bulbs are clothed upon with a miraculous raiment of loveliness. It is the time when myriads of unsuspected germs of life break forth into living green, and array themselves in gay and glistering garments. It is the time when the soft compelling breath of spring touches the withered and decaying trunks of ancient trees, and the magic sap travels up their gnarled and knotted frames and crowns them once again with glory of leaf and fruit. It is the time when the shepherd and the labourer find their pathways on field and hillside brave with shining flowers. It is the time when even the slum child's seeds in a broken flower-pot on a rusty balcony, where the rays of the sun are rare visitors, answer to the secret call to life and put forth bloom and fragrance. All this, God help us, we take for granted; and our modern souls are too full of the notion that it is scientifically explicable to surrender to the simple imperishable marvel and rapture of it. But we preachers have yet to learn that the greatest thing God ever does, is not when He spins His worlds in space, or regenerates the face of nature by the annual miracle of spring, but when human hearts cry out with unspeakable joy, "As for our

transgressions Thou shalt purge them away."
The Hand that can reach to the secret
springs of life, and purify them, washing
the stain from the conscience, and cleansing
the imagination of its pollutions, is engaged
in performing the most amazing miracle in
time. In the true church it is always spring-
time. From January to December is one season of regeneration. Revival is often thought
of as spasmodic and occasional; but that is
our fault. It is normal. The Resurrection
time is not at Easter alone. There is not a
moment of any day, in any year, when we
may not rise with Christ into newness of life,
and walk in His ways with transfigured
spirits. All this goes to make up the charm,
the fascination, the rapture, the romance of
the ministry.

The third point that I would emphasize is,
that *we are manifestly on the eve of new
applications of Christ's teaching, which will
revive the interest of the people in Christianity
to a surprising degree.* One of the most
remarkable features in the history of Christian progress during the past few years in

my own country, has been the creation of a new organization of a very simple character called "The Brotherhood Movement." It has attracted to itself hundreds of thousands of men ; and the secret of its attraction is twofold. Firstly, it presents for their acceptance a very simple faith, and secondly it brings them to close quarters with certain giant social evils which we of the churches have ignored too long. It may seem to some of you incredible, but it is literally true, that it came as a revelation to multitudes of men that Christianity had anything to say about poverty more than that all good Christian people ought to be charitable to the poor. Meanwhile, the poor themselves were inscribing on their banners "Justice not Charity," and when Christianity was carefully examined the surprising discovery was made that Christ Jesus and His apostles had much to say about Righteousness and Justice, and comparatively little to say about the duty of being charitable, save as it was included in the larger ideal.

The young preachers of recent years have

explored the contents of the word "Right-eousness," with the enthusiasm of pioneers opening up rich and fertile lands for the in-heritance of the future. Something has been happening even within the academic borders of our colleges. Men have been facing life as it is, and bringing it to the light of Christ. The social economist has invaded our quiet sanctuaries of religious thought with his dis-turbing facts and figures; and our young men have seen visions. The new compulsion has driven them down to the over-crowded areas where the disinherited of civilization make shift to exist; and the result has been that unique personal experience which changes scientific statistics into human facts. Is any one surprised that a new note can be detected in our preaching? Does any one marvel that young prophets are flinging down their challenge to society; and that features of industrialism which have been too long accepted as inevitable are to-day the objects of a fiery arraignment by men who are looking at them through eyes which Christ has purged and enlightened?

We are beginning to believe things which would have appalled our ancestors. We are beginning to believe that poverty need not exist; and that the restrictions upon human life and happiness, due to poverty, may be abolished. We see in the near future an almost indefinite elevation of the standard of living; and we throw the whole authority of Christianity into the scales in favour of the two great modern ideals, that work shall be equitably remunerated, and that wealth shall be equitably distributed.

After all it is not strange. Great causes always create a race of prophets. The watchword of the past century was Freedom. What orators the passion for Freedom created in this great land! Aye, and what martyrs for Freedom it made! The watchword of our new century is Justice. It will create as splendid an army of prophets; and it may very well be that before the victory is won, men and women will have to buy the new inheritance at a great price. But buy it they will; for the master passion in the breasts of the noblest of our young men is that the will of the Father shall be done "on earth as it is in heaven."

You will let me emphasize here a thought t' *t*, familiar as it is, must win an entrance into all your minds if you really mean *preaching*. Knowledge should be great wealth. But even as Mr. Ruskin used to teach that only such of our possessions as we well and truly use are well for us, or wealth; so it is with our treasures of knowledge. They only become mental wealth as they are efficiently and unselfishly used. Even the mere knowledge of Scripture may prove an arch deceiver. To know the names and the dates of the kings of Israel and Judah, is not necessarily to be a religious man; any more than to be able to answer Dr. Watts' catechism with all the proof texts, makes the youthful expert a true theologian. Science to-day is always with us, deluging us with statistics. Many a man has sought a reputation for philanthropy on the strength of his ability to quote columns of social facts. If your young student of medical and surgical science can label every bone in your anatomy, and dis-

course learnedly on the function of every
vital nerve, vein or tissue; if his knowledge
of the scientific facts of the human organism
is encyclopædic, he may, nevertheless, be as
far removed from being a true prophet in his
own sphere, as some dull and heavy bookman
is from being a great teacher. But if your
student of medicine and surgery be inspired
by a noble passion for humanity; if he is
ambitious to be able to keep the breadwinner
well for his work, to sustain the mother in
the hour of motherhood, to cherish childhood for the sake of its God-given possibilities, then he is in the way of becoming a
very prophet of health, and a living exponent
of the great saying of Paul that love re-
joiceth in the truth. Just in the same way
the mere accumulated facts as to human life
may produce a scholar rather than a seer.
All the social statistics ever compiled in the
new sociological laboratories may only prove
an incubus upon the mind, and a darkening
of counsel. I have known parliaments, as
well as churches, as intimidated by statistics
as the ten craven-hearted spies were cowed

by the walled cities of Canaan and the stature
of the sons of the Anakim. There has come
the ringing cry of some one with the divine
genius of faith, " Let us go up against them,
for we are well able to overcome them," and
somehow the walls of Jericho have fallen, and
impossibilities have melted away like the
mists of morning. So we are beginning to
see, beneath the baptism of our new Pentecost, that our vast inexorable problems, compounded of prejudices, vested interests, and
ancient wrongs are by no means as impreg-
nable as they look. But they constitute a
supreme appeal to faith, and to what I may
call Christian patriotism.

The preacher who is going forth unto the
battle-field to-day for the kingdom of God on
earth, will enter the fray to hearkening strains
of music. The Church of Christ to-day does
not despair of calling into existence a Christian civilization. It refuses to acquiesce in
the permanence of those social vices and social wrongs that have entrenched themselves
so deeply even under the visible authority of
the Cross. There is arising an army of young

knights of Christ who have taken sacramental vows, that none of their brethren shall
have to live in the future under conditions
that are fatal alike to physical health and to
even a moderate standard of chastity and
honour. They have vowed that the cruel
exigencies of a merciless competition shall
not always kill the truth and self-respect of
those who are taken in its toils. They are
resolved that the progress of humanity shall
be something better and nobler than an un-
relieved struggle for existence ; and men
something diviner than

> " Dragons of the prime
> That tare each other in their slime."

They are resolved—" highly resolved," as
Lincoln used to say—that the slum and the
sweater shall vanish from the face of this
earth which Christ's feet once trod, and His
deathless love forever sanctifies. They are
resolved that men and women shall not always be subjected to the legion of temptations that centre in the gaming hell and the
saloon. They are resolved that human conditions of labour and life, in the factory and

on the land, shall be substituted for conditions which made health and happiness almost impossible. In other words, they have caught the glow of the idealism of the great Jewish prophets who saw in vision the Messianic age, and hailed it as the destined day of God.

I am not here to urge you to identify yourselves with any particular school of economics or politics. I am one of those who can honestly claim, that I can count the political sermons I have preached in twenty-five years on the fingers of one hand. But that has been because I have taken other and more unconventional opportunities of dealing with great national issues, as they have arisen in my own country. But I hold that that man's soul is dead, and he is thereby incapacitated for the office of preacher, who is insensitive to the great human movements that are advancing in every land, and that have for their object the throwing wide open of the doors of opportunity to all citizens, so as to make possible for every worker a decent competence, and for every child the fullest measure of culture of which it is capable. Possibly some of the things that I am venturing to say to you, are leading me on to dangerous ground. If so, I must take the risk. This is not a plea for any special set of opinions ; but it is a plea for wide and generous social sympathies, and such clear and courageous outlook as gave to the Hebrew prophets the religious leadership of their generation.

My fourth point is, that *over this world of military camps, bristling frontiers and armoured fleets, there is being heard to-day with new insistence the ever-romantic strains of the angels' song of Peace and Goodwill.* The Gospel has a twofold mission. It is ours to break down the barriers between man and God, and it is ours to break down the barriers between man and man. Nobody can calculate the effect on the life of this world, if every minister of Christ were to know himself charged with full authority as an ambassador of peace, and were to make it a definite part of his mission to plead the cause of brotherhood with all other peoples. No governments could resist such concerted appeal. The Church of Christ can, if she will,

make the Hague Tribunal the centre of the
world's hopes. In my honest judgment, unless the Church brings this era of militarism
to a close, and exorcises the demons of hated,
suspicion and aggression, there is no power
that can. And it is right in the line of the
missionary crusade. It is but obedience to
marching orders, after all. I want to appeal
to you to include this definitely in your
military accoutrement—this fighting faith in
a world subject to reason and justice because
Christ-ruled. I ask you to believe that no
ideal of organized Peace is too extravagant
or ambitious to stand within your horizon.
To-day, all the dreams of science, which were
discredited and derided for generations by
that much overrated quality called common-
sense, are coming true. The children of
faith and imagination have had revealed unto
them what was hidden from the sapient and
prudent.

" The Heavens fill with commerce, argosies of magic
        sails,
    Pilots of the purple twilight, dropping down with
        costly bales."

Science's predictions are coming true; science's splendid faith is being justified. The impossible is happening before our eyes. The sages are being confounded; and, as always happens, the seers are triumphing, and the visionaries and the idealists are seen to be the supremely practical people. But we are still short-sighted; at odds with the man who sees a stage further than we can. Mr. Arnold Bennett's inventor is full of scorn for the man who is the mere slave of yesterday and who will not believe that a wooden ship must give way to an iron ship, but he is equally scornful of the heir of to-morrow who perceives that an iron ship must give way to a steel ship. But the most urgent question of our day is whether moral progress is going to keep pace with material progress.

" If we trod the deeps of ocean, if we struck the stars
  in rising,
 If we wrapt the globe intently with one hot electric
  breath,
  'Twere but power within our tether, no new spirit-
   power comprising,
 And in life we were not greater men nor bolder men
  in death."

We hail the realized hopes and dreams of
science, but shall the higher science arrive
with her material miracles, and is there to
be nothing but defeat and despair for the
higher morality ?   Shall Reason win the day
in every sphere except where her victories
would be most fruitful ?   Shall we erase from
the canvas of the future the most glowing of
all visions—the day of Humanity

" When the war-drum throbs no longer, and the bat-
　　tle-flags are furled
　In the Parliament of man, the Federation of the
　　world."

Who will say that man shall ride upon the
wings of the wind, and talk across the empty
spaces of ocean from ship to ship and from
shore to shore, and yet shall not conquer the
selfishness, mistrust and hatred in his own
heart?   Who will say that he shall vanquish
every physical disease, only to be conquered
by the venom of malice, envy and suspicion
that poisons the veins of his own soul ?   No,
if you do your duty, the progress in the
world's idealism shall keep pace with her
advance in material prosperity ; and the

Church's early ideal of internationalism shall be realized, with its glorious consequences in the deliverance of the weary nations from the burdens beneath which they groan; and the emancipation of the human spirit everywhere, from those dark shadows of mistrust and fear which have been the perpetual nightmare of the past.

I have done. It remains only for me to congratulate you on your birthright. You are born to an inheritance in a great and splendid age. All the Christian centuries offer you their hoarded wealth. For you every prophet has prophesied until now; for you the martyrs suffered, and the saints glorified God in shining lives of holy love and service. For you the poets have sung, and at your feet every one of the world-thinkers has laid the harvest of his brain. For the last hundred years Science has been weaving its wizard spells about this earth, and drawing us all nearer and nearer together, so that we may contribute what is best in our life to the common stock of the world's wealth.

Into this magnificent heritage you have been born; and into the full possession of it you are about to enter. My advice to you is, in a word, "Belong to your century." "Hold fast that which thou hast, that no man take thy crown." To be alive here and now, with the call of God in your souls, and the widening opportunities of to-day at your doors, is indeed to have been crowned by Heaven. Let no man discrown you. Do not live in the past. Do not let the glamour of days and events gone by seduce you from your loyalty to the present hour. Whatever faults may be chargeable to our century, it is the best century for you and me. That is why I appeal to you with all affection and solemnity. "*To-day*, oh, that ye would hear His voice!" The voice of God in the life of *to-day!*

I have recalled to you, in the course of these lectures, some of the memorable words and deeds of those whose names are inscribed in letters of gold on the roll of the Church's leaders and prophets. It would have been a great thing no doubt to have run with Timothy on some errand for St. Paul. It would

have been a great thing to have dared everything for Christ when Nero was on the throne.
It would have been a great thing to have
confronted emperors with Athanasius, to have
died for freedom with Savonarola, to have
crossed the Atlantic with Brewster and Brad-
ford, to have waked the world to new spiritual life with Whitefield and Wesley.   But let
no man say that our age is inferior in opportunity to any that has gone before.   The one
demand is the consecrated spirit, and the forward mind.

It will belong to your ministry to conserve
for the men and women of to-day the eternal
truths in which our fathers lived, but to present those truths as they have passed through
the living mind and been shined upon by the
broadening light, that is the precious gift of
God to our generation.   I think perhaps this
ministry of yours can be best realized from
that description of the conversation between
the prophet Brand and his wife Agnes, that
we owe to the genius of Ibsen.

Brand says :

" Oftentimes my light is low,
Dim my reason, dull my thought,
And there seems a kind of gladness
In immeasurable sadness.
In such hours as these I see
God, as at no other, near;
Oh, so near, it seems to me
I could speak and He would hear.
Like a lost child then I long
To be folded to His heart,
And be gathered by His strong
Tender Father-arms to rest."

And Agnes says :

" Brand, oh see Him so alway !
To thy supplication near —
God of love and not of fear."

But Brand replies :

" No, I may not bar His way,
Nor run counter to my call;
I must see Him, vast, sublime
As the Heavens,—a pigmy Time,
Needs a giant God withal ! "

" Oh ! but thou mayst see Him near,
See Him as a Father dear,
Bow thy head upon His breast,
There, when thou art weary, rest,
Then, return, with face aglow
From His presence, fair and free,
Bear His glory down to me
Worn with battle-thrust and throe ! "

It is given, I think, to the prophet of to-day to combine a great sense of God's majesty and might with an equal sense of His nearness and fathomless love. The mighty God is the Everlasting Father, and we must preach the Gospel so. As Browning says:

" I who saw Power see now Love perfect too ! "

There is no more to be said. Let us have courage. Our mission is to inspire men ; and in Christ is inexhaustible inspiration ; and revelation that is always new. In Mr. Henry James' masterpiece "Roderick Hudson," there is the clever successful artist Gloriani, who has sold his soul to make money, and grown cynical as to the transaction. He thinks the true inspiration of genius is but a fickle thing, and few if any can afford to pay the price. " My dear fellow," he says to the real artist who is suffering from temporary eclipse of faith, " passion burns out, inspiration runs to seed. Some fine day every artist finds himself sitting face to face with his lump of clay, with his empty canvas, with his sheet of blank paper, waiting in vain for the revelation to be made, for the Muse to descend. He must learn to do without the Muse. When the fickle jade forgets her way to your studio don't waste any time in tearing your hair and meditating suicide. Come round and see me, and I will show you how to console yourself."

Many has been the minister who has thought and felt like that. He sees himself sitting before a blank sheet of paper, waiting in vain for the sermon that will not come. He thinks that, if not now, yet a score of years on, his inspiration may have "run to seed." What is he to do? Is he "to learn to do without the Muse"? Is he to "console himself" by some lower ideal and come to regard himself as a hireling, and to look upon his work as a profession and a livelihood? God forbid. We cannot do without the spirit—without the inspiration. Without that mystic light and power, our art is indeed barren and contemptible. But, remember, our inspiration includes all others. Nature, Poetry, Art, Literature, Life—we

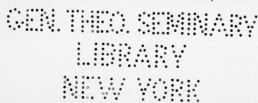

have the freedom of all the schools. And above and beyond all others, we have the school of Christ. No minister shall ever be bankrupt of a message who is living in that Society. The jaded brain may sometimes refuse its office. We may feel some Sunday evening as if we had fired our last shot. But there is still for the child of faith a cruse of oil and a barrel of meal, that mystically do not fail.

The miracle of our calling is that they who wait upon the Lord renew their strength. We may not always mount up on wings as eagles, nor is it well we should. But by the grace of God vouchsafed to us we can run and not be weary; we can walk—briskly, one hopes!—and not faint. In the splendid certainty of inspiration which is the gift of a God whose gifts are "without repentance," may you accept your ministry at your Master's hands; and living in the dignity and the glory of it, serve your generation, by the will of God, before you fall asleep!

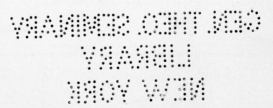